# The Church in a Society of Abundance

# THE CHURCH IN A
# SOCIETY OF ABUNDANCE

❧ edited by Arthur E. Walmsley

NEW YORK
1963

*CE*
*261./*W
W|62

152160

Copyright © 1963 by The Seabury Press, Incorporated
Library of Congress Catalog Card Number: 63-9058
Design by Nancy H. Dale
Printed in the United States of America
430-863-C-4.5

## ❧ ACKNOWLEDGMENTS

Grateful acknowledgment is made to the following for permission to reprint the copyrighted papers indicated:

*Bulletin of the Atomic Scientists* for Surendra J. Patel's "The Threat of Annihilation."

Center for the Study of Democratic Institutions, The Fund for the Republic, for David Horowitz's "The Threats of Stagnation and Starvation."

*Christianity and Crisis* for Kenneth Underwood's "Social Ethic in the New Era."

# ❧ TO WILLIAM SCARLETT

## Bishop, Teacher, and Prophet

## ❧ FOREWORD

It is a cliché to say that we live in a time of rapid social change. But it happens to be true. It is equally obvious to add that in the United States of America we live amidst great material abundance though other parts of the world lack even a minimum standard of living. There is, then, special need for American Christians to take a hard, realistic look at the land in which they live and at the world of which it is an integral part.

It is not only that the current situation presents obvious problems, but Christians believe that God works in and through human history. Christians believe that we are responsible for that part of God's creation which has been entrusted to us. Christians dare to believe that we are not passively to conform to the world that is, but rather that, with the help of the grace of God, we are to work to transform it.

This book leads the reader to take such a look at the world and at himself within this world. It follows in the great tradition of *Christianity Takes a Stand*, which was written under the guiding inspiration of Bishop William Scarlett, a Christian of magnificent vision. Like that former volume, this book was initiated by the Joint Commission of the Church in Human Affairs of the General Convention of the Protestant Episcopal Church in the United States of America. That Commission is composed of lay women and men, priests, and bishops of the

Episcopal Church. The Department of Christian Social Relations of the Episcopal Church has cooperated wholeheartedly. The Rev. Arthur E. Walmsley, executive secretary of the Division of Christian Citizenship of that Department, has not only served as editor but has also written a stimulating chapter.

There is a logical rightness in linking beginnings and endings. So perhaps in this Foreword, which we write with appreciation, we can do no better than to quote from the Epilogue of the book:

A new age has come into being, one in which the potential of inflicting limitless suffering is as real to men as the promise of a new abundance. That God has placed such potential in human hands is either a divine caprice of unbelievable cruelty—or a mark of infinite love and trust. The vocation of Christians in our day, as in any other, is to discern the love and justice and judgment of God in the life of the world and to witness to his power. Within the disciplined discovery of the action of God in the world of economic, social, and political life will emerge the patterns of church life appropriate to the new era.

To that "disciplined discovery" this book is devoted.

THE RT. REV. C. GRESHAM MARMION, JR.
*Chairman,* Joint Commission of the
Church in Human Affairs
THE RT. REV. FREDERICK J. WARNECKE
*Chairman,* Editorial Committee

# ❧ CONTENTS

# The Church in a Society of Abundance

# ➔ INTRODUCTION

In September, 1961, the General Convention of the Protestant Episcopal Church met in Detroit, Michigan, a city which as much as any other symbolizes the achievements of modern industrial society and the revolution in technology which have made it possible. Through the imagination of members of the Convention's Joint Commission on the Church in Human Affairs, the larger part of a working day of the Convention was devoted to an examination of how industrial society confronts the Church's ministry. Beginning with an early-morning tour of industrial centers and discussions with members of management, the unions, and workers themselves, upwards of eight hundred bishops, deputies, and others attending the Convention returned to Cobo Hall for a showing of a specially prepared film on the problems of daily work and decision-making in the modern corporation. This was followed by presentations from a leading sociologist and a priest serving a major industrial center.

How well is the Church doing in industrial America? How much are we in touch with the problems raised by rapid technological change? by automation? by the nature of the cor-

porate structure? These questions were barely raised in the
Convention program. This volume of essays continues the
examination.

Its premise is that we have moved, in the last generation,
into a new society, brought on by a scientific-technological
revolution. The marks of this society are most conspicuous in
the United States and Western Europe, but the whole world
is caught in the process. The revolution is basic, changing not
only man's relation to production and consumption of goods,
but the face of the city, the relation of government to its people, and the structure of the family itself. Popular imagination
can hardly conceive the long-range implications of the revolution, and phrases such as "affluent society" or "automation"
mystify rather than enlighten.

In only one area, the sociology of urban life, has there been
any significant body of literature written with the Church's
problems in mind. This writing has tended to pose the dilem-
mas of the institutional church in the changing city more than
it has explored in depth what is happening to men, women,
and children faced with the stresses of an urban industrial culture. There are, to be sure, thoughtful clergy and lay persons
in a wide range of disciplines struggling with what technological and scientific breakthrough means for the life of the
Church. But the pace of change is constantly accelerating, and
the new conditions which confront us are so basic that the
Church today finds itself in a missionary situation not unlike
that of entering an entirely strange society, in which the missionary is confronted with new institutions, new language, and
people whose life is shaped by thought patterns alien to the
world the missionary grew in.

The book is in three sections. Part I is a survey of some of the marks of the abundant society. Kenneth E. Boulding describes "The Society of Abundance." In Chapter 2, John V. P. Lassoe, Jr., considers the problems of "Man and Society in the New Era." Kenneth Underwood, in Chapter 3, discusses "Social Ethic in the New Era." Chapter 4, written by the editor of the volume, examines "The Mission of the Church in the New Era." These four papers attempt to outline briefly something of the changed situation conjured by the words "society of abundance."

Part II is an examination of two overarching threats to the society of abundance. David Horowitz writes on "The Threats of Stagnation and Starvation," the problem of distribution of human abundance. Surendra J. Patel writes on "The Threat of Annihilation," the economic cost of the arms race.

Part III is a consideration of three problems confronting the Church's ministry in this new era. In "Leisure in the New Era," Cameron P. Hall poses the challenge put to Christian teaching by a shift from an economy of production to one of consumption. "Stewardship: Private and Public" by Ross M. Robertson examines the relation of the Church's ministry to human need against the increasing role played by government. "The Recovery of Ministry in the New Era" by Franklin H. Littell probes ways by which the Church is seeking to engage the principalities and powers of the age of abundance.

THE EDITOR

# ⥤ PART I
# The New Era

# I

## THE SOCIETY OF ABUNDANCE

### by Kenneth E. Boulding

The most important changes in the condition of mankind are probably the long, steady transitions in which there is a slow but persistent development in one direction in some central variable over a long period of years. Changes of this kind, like the growth of a plant, are not easy to perceive, and our image of man's history is frequently colored by the more dramatic changes such as wars and revolutions which take place quickly, but which may not be so important in their long-run effect, because they do not have a consistent direction.

For the past three hundred years or so, man has been subject to long, persistent change which I have called elsewhere "the second great transition." The first great transition was, of course, the passing from precivilized to civilized societies, which began with the invention of agriculture and the domestication of livestock perhaps eight thousand years ago, and which culminated in the development of political and coercive skills which concentrated the fruits of agriculture into cities. This also was a long, slow process extending over hundreds and, indeed, thousands of years. We are now in the middle of a change in the

9

state of man certainly as large as and perhaps even larger than the transition from precivilized to civilized societies. In order to dramatize this stage I have sometimes described it as a change from civilized to postcivilized society. If this word is too shocking because of our long association of civilization with the good society, we can call the new state of man into which we are moving the "developed" society.

Whatever we call it, we must recognize that the developed society is as different from the society of classical civilization as classical civilization was from the precivilized societies which preceded it. What we call, rather innocuously, "economic development" is nothing more than an enormous revolution in the state of man, perhaps the greatest revolution which he has so far undergone. The spectrum of human societies is of course fairly continuous, and any classification is somewhat arbitrary; nevertheless, the grouping into savage, civilized, and developed societies is at least a workable starting point.

The key variable in explaining the transition from one of these states to the next is the efficiency of human labor in producing the basic needs of subsistence, that is, in providing the essential energy requirements of the human organism. Food is the most important element in the means of subsistence, while shelter and clothing, by cutting down calorie loss, are also important. If we take the family as the basic unit, we may say that precivilized, or savage societies are characterized by the fact that it takes a family roughly full time to produce the means of subsistence for itself, and it produces no surplus over and above what it must consume in order to stay alive and to reproduce. This seems to be the case in most food-gathering or hunting-and-fishing societies. With the invention of agriculture and the domestication of crops and livestock, it became possible for a single family to produce more subsistence than it needed to keep itself alive and reproducing. This surplus of the means of subsistence is not in itself a sufficient condition to produce civilization, though it is a necessary one. Obviously the cities cannot be fed unless the food provider produces more food than he and his family can eat. Cities and civilization, however, are the product of the agricultural food surplus plus a political organization usually involving some coercive means which can extract the food surplus from the food producer and use it to feed the kings, armies, priests, philosophers, and artisans who make up and construct the city. The surplus upon which classical civilizations were built was astonishingly small. Even at the height of the Roman Empire, for instance, which may be taken as the ideal type of classical civilization, it probably took about 75 per cent of the population to feed the total, which meant that only 25 per cent could be spared for urban employments. This is still the case today in those countries of the world that are regarded as underdeveloped, such as Indonesia, which is about at the level of development of the Roman Empire at its height. It is hard for us, especially those who are nurtured in the traditions of classical education, to think of the Roman Empire as a poor country, but in fact its population, extent, and per-capita income were probably similar to those of present-day Indonesia, which is one of the poorest countries in the world.

The technology of classical civilization is largely a "folk" technology; it is based on the slow accumulation of traditional knowledge which is transmitted primarily through the family. Even the beginnings of science in Babylonia and Greece affected the technologies of these societies very little. Folk technology, however, has a limited horizon. It does not involve

much division of labor in the learning process; it tends to be
conservative and rigid; and it is not surprising, therefore, that
once the step from precivilized to civilized society has been
made there are still long periods of technological stagnation.
The early civilization of the Indus at Mohenjo-Daro appears to
have been technologically stagnant for almost a thousand years,
and even the Roman Empire seems to have stagnated from the
time of Augustus to that of Constantine. It was, indeed, the
fall of the Roman Empire in the West that laid the foundation
for the next technological advance. The so-called Dark Ages,
from the fifth to the tenth centuries in Western Europe, saw
such fundamental inventions as the water wheel, the stirrup,
the horse collar, and the rudder, none of which the Romans
had.

The origins of the second great transition, like all origins, are
obscure. It has been attributed to, among others, the Benedictines of the sixth century A.D., who pioneered in certain
aspects of agricultural and mechanical technology. The suggestion here is that the Benedictines were the first intellectuals
who worked with their hands. The technological stagnation of
classical civilization depends in part on the sharp separation between the intellectual and the manual laborer. In a society
where the life of the mind is supported by the labor of slaves,
there is no incentive either on the part of the slave or on the
part of the master to improve the efficiency of labor. It was
only as Christianity raised labor to a dignity which it did not
possess in classical times or in the great Asian civilizations that
the possibility of improving the efficiency of labor by taking
thought first entered the world. A considerable part of the explanation of the great historic difference between the development of Asia and of Europe may lie in the fact that, whereas

the religious teachers of Asia were princes and philosophers, Jesus was a carpenter and St. Paul was a tentmaker. Christianity was the first proletarian religion, and because of this, even when it reached power and affluence, it still found a place for physical labor as an activity consistent with the dignity and purpose of man—*laborare est orare*.

Whatever its origins, from about the sixth century on we can detect the beginnings of a long, slow, but persistent increase in the productivity of labor, partly, as Adam Smith observed, arising out of the specialization of labor itself, but more importantly arising out of the activity of "philosophers or men of speculation whose trade it is not to do anything, but to observe everything, and who upon that account are often capable of combining together the powers of the most distant and dissimilar objects." [1]

By the seventeenth century the movement which only the utmost refinements of historical hindsight can perceive in the Dark Ages comes in full view. "God said, 'Let Newton be,' and there was light." Science, like a chain reaction, develops as an enormous and irreversible expansion in human knowledge, extending its domain to one field after another. Hand in hand with the explosion of knowledge comes a similar explosion of know-how. New sources of energy—steam in the eighteenth century, electricity in the nineteenth, atomic energy in the twentieth—give man enormous new powers. The story is familiar and need not be recapitulated. What is happening here, however, is a long, steady increase in the productivity of human effort, mainly because of man's ability to learn and to teach. We see this manifested dramatically in agriculture. In classical civilization, as we have seen, it took three-quarters of the people to feed the whole; in modern America we can produce all the food we need with 10 per cent of the population, perhaps even with 5 per cent, thus releasing more than 90 per cent to produce the conveniences and luxuries of life.

It is important to realize that we are still in the middle of this transition and there are no signs as yet of its impetus diminishing. If anything, we seem to be in the accelerating phase of the change, and it is probable that we have not yet reached the midpoint. We have only begun, for instance, to devote substantial resources to research and development itself. Much of the development of the previous centuries was on a haphazard and almost accidental basis, and involved an astonishingly small amount of actual human resources. Today we are devoting billions of dollars to the explicit purpose of technical change. We may not be doing this very wisely, but even the most wasteful application of resources of this kind can hardly fail to produce substantial results. We often gain the impression, from the way history is taught, that the Industrial Revolution was something that happened in the eighteenth century. Nothing could be further from the truth. The eighteenth century saw some quickening of the rate of change, though it could be argued that the increase of the rate of change has been fairly steady from the sixth century on and that the eighteenth century represents no great watershed. This we can leave the historians to dispute. What is indisputable is that the revolution in the state of man which is due to science and technology is a process still continuing at an accelerated pace, and the end is nowhere in sight. The wildest excesses of science fiction are probably not adequate to describe the possible state of man which may emerge from this enormous transition.

Merely because we have been observing a long and steady historical process extending over some hundreds of years, with only occasional reversals, it is tempting to fall into the belief that this process is automatic and irreversible. This belief would be a dangerous illusion. Any trend, no matter how long it has been going on, is the result of certain underlying conditions, and if these conditions change, the trend can come to an end or be reversed. There are a number of pitfalls which lie in the path of the second great transition, and it is by no means a foregone conclusion that man will achieve the society of abundance toward which he seems now to be moving. The most obvious pitfall is the possibility of nuclear war, which could easily be an irretrievable disaster. Even if we avoid general nuclear war, the continuance of the present arms race and, still more, its extension represent a burden on the back of mankind which may, in the long run, make all the difference between achieving the abundant society or falling back into an even more primitive state than man's present condition. The world-war industry now consumes resources estimated at about $120 billion a year; this is equal to the total income of the poorest half of the world's population. Even though some of this goes into research and development, which spills over into civilian and humane uses, the bulk of it from the point of view of the development of mankind as a whole is sheer waste—and it is a waste which we cannot afford.

The second pitfall along the road of the transition is the inability of man to control the growth of his own population. At the present rate of reproduction we will reach "standing room only" in a little over seven hundred years, and long before that time there will have to be a drastic change. Technology alone cannot exorcise the Malthusian demon. If the only thing that can check the growth of population is misery, then no matter how advanced our technology the ultimate end is merely to permit a larger population to live in misery. This is what I sometimes call "the utterly dismal theorem." The conscious control of population, however, in a way that is consistent with human dignity and privacy is still an unsolved problem. At present the price of population control is high, no matter how it is approached. The two countries of the world that seem to have been most successful in restricting the growth of population are Ireland and Japan. In Ireland this is achieved by late marriages and a strict Puritan-Catholic culture that imposes strong sanctions against sexual indulgence. In Japan the solution seems to be through abortion, though in both countries there is a strong familistic morality. Whatever the price of population control, it will eventually have to be paid, and we should be concerned to see that the price be as low as possible.

The third pitfall along the road to the abundant society is the possible failure to achieve a permanent high-level technology. The high incomes of the twentieth century have been achieved largely by drawing on our geological capital in the form of fossil fuels (coal, oil, gas) and ores. This means that our present technology is ultimately suicidal, and that, indeed, if we do not move to another technical level, the more economic development we have in the undeveloped parts of the world, the sooner will come the evil day when all geological capital is gone and all mines and wells are exhausted. If by that time we have not achieved a permanent high-level technology, man will have to step back into a technology based on what the earth can grow by the use of current solar energy. Whether this permanent technology is high-level or low-level depends in large measure on the use we are making of the present opportunity.

Fortunately there are signs that a permanent high-level technology, released from dependence on geological capital, is at least just below our horizon. To the present time, the economic system has been mainly "entropic," in the sense that man has taken stores of energies of concentrated materials and has dissipated and diffused these in seas and in dumps throughout the world. The soil, the seas, and the atmosphere are the only permanent sources from which man can draw what materials he needs. Two technical developments of the twentieth century—one the Haber process for the fixation of nitrogen from the air, and the other the Dow process of extracting magnesium from the sea—point toward a new kind of technology in which we will be able to use energy in order to concentrate the diffuse materials of the ocean and the atmosphere. This may ultimately release us from dependence on exhaustible mines. At the moment, however, we are putting very little energy into research and development in these areas, and it may be that we do not have much time. Geologically speaking, the whole present era of extraction of fuels and ores is only a flash in the pan, a mere moment of time. It may be a moment, however, long enough to permit man to transform the stored resources of the earth into knowledge and information which will enable him to dispense with them. The present time must be regarded as a unique moment in the history of this planet. We have at most a few centuries to make the transition to a permanent high-level technology, and if we fail to do this, man will fall back to scratching a meager living from the soil in an exhausted and mined-out world. The critical nature of the present time makes one all the more resentful of the resources wasted in the world-war industry and makes disarmament one of the major priorities of man.

It may well be that when we see this second great transition in its perspective, we shall perceive in it not one revolution but

two: the second, however, following so close upon the heels of
the first that they seem to be part of the same process. The first
might be called the "energy revolution," and the second the
"information revolution." The energy revolution is perhaps the
more obvious, and certainly the per-capita use of energy in a
society for human concerns correlates well with its per-capita
income. If in modern America per-capita incomes are of the
order of twenty times what they were in classical civilization,
a major explanation of this phenomenon is that Americans use
so much more energy per head. Insofar as this energy is derived
from fossil fuels, or even from uranium, it is not, as we have
seen, capable of sustaining a high-level society indefinitely.
While it lasts, however, our riches are clearly due to it. It is a
commonplace that one modern man has a hundred mechanical
horses to do his will. The growth of abundance follows the
ability to utilize different forms of energy other than man's
muscles: first, livestock, including human slaves; then the wind
and moving water; then coal, oil, and, finally, atomic fission.
The permanent high-level society will probably have to be based
either on the energy released by fusion or on the use of solar
energy, which is practically the same thing.

Energy, however, is not the whole story. Life uses energy to
segregate entropy, that is, to build up more and more complex
structures with less randomness, more order and structure, and
less probability than the world around them, at the cost of
increasing disorder elsewhere. Society does likewise, and the
high-level society uses its energy in order to create little islands
of diminished randomness and increased structure: food,
homes, cities, art, and religion. The information revolution is
a revolution in the efficiency of the teaching-learning process
and the spread of knowledge—knowledge being to information

what capital is to income. The major information revolution of the first great change was the invention of writing, which enormously increased man's power of communication across time and space and permitted the organization of empires and the development of history in the consciousness of man, by liberating mankind from the impermanence of the spoken word. The invention of printing played somewhat the same role in the second great transition as the invention of writing did in the first. It permitted a great increase in the diffusion of knowledge, and hence paved the way for the scientific revolution which followed it. Science itself, however, is now the major source of the information revolution. It is a relatively small subculture based on an extensive communication and learning process of a peculiar kind. In folk culture the basic image of the world is stable. For unnumbered generations, for instance, the Navajo believed that rain dances would cause rain. The image of the world is stable in spite of disappointments partly because it is reinforced with the coercive powers of sacredness, but also because disappointments can usually be explained away. If we perform a rain dance and it does not rain, there must have been something wrong with the dance; and as rain dances are very complicated, a careful searching of the heart and the memory will usually find something wrong with them. In a folk culture, therefore, whatever happens tends to confirm one's image of the world. If the image is that rain dances cause rain—which is, incidentally, a scientific proposition whether true or not, that is, a testable proposition about the empirical world—then in a folk culture almost everything that happens confirms the image. If, following a rain dance, it does rain, this of course confirms the belief that rain dances cause rain; if it does not rain, the dance is examined, something wrong is found, and thus also is confirmed the belief that a rain dance *properly performed* causes rain.

There is enough similarity here to what goes on in a science laboratory—where the student is expected to make the experiment come out right, and where, if it does not come out right, the assumption is that there was something wrong with the experiment—to make us a little uneasy about the sociology of the scientific community. Nevertheless, by and large the success of science is the result of the fact that, by contrast with folk culture, in the scientific subculture the image of the world is not stable, and disappointment or failure of experience to correspond with what our image of the world led us to expect, results not in a rejection of the experience or a rejection of the inference which led to the expectation, but rather in a readjustment of the image of the world itself. An experiment may be little more than a simplified rain dance, but the fact that it is simplified is all-important. If the experiment turns out unexpectedly, as did the famous Michelson-Morley experiment on the velocity of light, we cannot deny the experience or the inference, and hence we must reorganize our image of the world.

One of the most significant developments of the last one or two hundred years is that the energy revolution, or the increase in the per-capita use of energy, has come increasingly to depend on the information revolution, that is, on the scientific subculture. The domestication of animals, the invention of the horse collar, even the invention of the wheel, the water wheel, and the windmill, possibly the early steam engines, grew out of folk culture. It is extremely unlikely, however, that the folk culture could have discovered electricity, and it is impossible that it could have discovered atomic energy. Indeed, we can say that the information revolution has taken command and that the energy revolution now depends on it.

The information revolution, furthermore, has aspects which are significant for economic abundance and which go beyond the mere provision of more energy. In the past generation we have seen the development on an astonishing scale of information-processing and problem-solving machines, that is, computers. The development of the high-speed electronic computer is likely to have an impact on human life and organization at least equal to that produced by the inventions of writing or printing. It is not impossible, indeed, that the long-run impact will be greater than that of any previous change in the organization of the information process. Nonhuman sources of energy increase abundance by adding power, as it were, to the human muscle; nonhuman information-processing and problem-solving machines increase abundance by adding power to the human mind. The importance of this is clear. It is mind, not muscle, that produces abundance; the elephant has a lot more muscle than man, but in the absence of man it has no means of harnessing energy outside its own muscular system because its mind (that is, its information-processing and problem-solving system) cannot go much beyond its muscular environment. It is the glory and the peril of man that his mind has leaped far beyond the environment of his own body to take in the secrets both of the stars and of the atoms. With what might be called the folk powers of his mind he perceived the value of fire, he harnessed animals to his will, and he harnessed the winds and the waters. Now, because of the information revolution, he can expand the powers of his own mind. A computer is to a mind what, say, a power saw is to a muscle. It does not replace it or even compete with it, but it enormously expands its capability.

The development of automation in industry is but one phase of this information revolution and in the long run perhaps not even the most important phase. It does represent, however, a movement which is going to have a substantial impact on the developed economies, especially, in the course of the next generation. The production of commodities involves the application of both energy and information to the earth in order to change the form of its materials from a less structured to a more structured form. In primitive craftsmanship man provides both the energy and the information for this process out of the resources of his own body alone; this is the boy whittling a stick or primitive man shaping an arrowhead. Man soon begins to shape things into tools which economize the use of his energy. Then, as we have seen, he begins to draw on nonhuman sources of energy which further increase the productivity of his effort. Now he is at the stage of economizing on the information process itself, which gives him, as it were, an additional leverage. Aristotle's vision of the shuttle that moves by itself and the lyre that plays itself has already largely come to pass. The extension of human powers in information-processing and problem-solving is something, again, of which we have seen only the beginning, and we cannot prophesy its end.

Even though we cannot see the end of this great process, we have a certain obligation to look twenty-five or fifty years ahead to ponder the kind of society likely to be emerging by that time. It is clearly a society in which the whole structure of human activity is very different from what it was in classical civilization, or even from what it is now. In classical civilization roughly

80 per cent of the population was in agriculture or other rural pursuits and about 20 per cent in all other occupations. In the United States today we have a little over 10 per cent in agriculture, about 30 per cent in manufacturing, and about 60 per cent in what might be called the "tertiary" occupations—the professions, trades, and so on. There is little doubt that this trend will continue, and in fifty years we may reasonably expect—short of disaster—to have all our food produced by perhaps 5 per cent of the population or less; to be producing all our manufactured goods with perhaps 15 or 20 per cent; and to have 75 per cent at least of the population in tertiary occupations. There are some who quail before this prospect and who visualize automation as producing massive and intractable unemployment. This view seems to me mistaken; I see no reason why, given proper economic policy, we cannot employ as many people as we wish. We are moving rapidly toward what we might call a service economy in which a relatively small proportion of the labor force will produce all the "things" that we need, and the great bulk of us will be providing services for each other. Nobody as yet has spelled out in detail what an economy of this kind would really look like and exactly what we would do for each other. To what extent, for instance, would we expand professional services? To what extent would we expand the more unskilled services? One of the worrisome problems of an economy of this type is what happens to the demand for the labor of the unskilled and those who are not capable of acquiring skill. The economy into which we are moving seems to demand a high level of education and skill from almost everybody, and unskilled and untrained labor is rapidly diminishing in importance. It is disquieting, for instance, that the general rate of unemployment, while too high

to be comfortable, is not too high to be tolerable; when we examine this carefully we find that unemployment is largely concentrated among the unskilled Negroes and among youth, especially unskilled youth. We may find ourselves by the year 2000 with a society in which there is no place for the unskilled or the untrainable, and how we give these people the moral status which their position as fellow human beings demands may turn out to be one of the major ethical problems of our day.

In spite of these difficulties I am prepared to assert that the balance sheet of the information revolution on the whole is enormously positive. Furthermore, there is no retreat; there is no way back to Eden. Once we have eaten of the tree of knowledge, a flaming sword bars our return to the innocence which is born of ignorance. Because there is no road back to Eden, the only way that we can take is forward to Zion—toward the great hope which man has always had of a kingdom of heaven on earth. We can discern the outlines of Zion more clearly perhaps than any previous generation, and it has become for us more than an eschatological hope or even a utopian dream; it has become a city set on the hill of the future toward which there now seems to be a road.

The road, as we have seen, is strewn with pitfalls. Nevertheless, our ability to avoid the pitfalls depends in large measure on the continued progress of the information revolution. The achievement of stable peace and disarmament depends on the accomplishment of a certain intellectual task in the understanding of international systems and of an educational task in modifying men's images of the world. The solution of the population problem likewise depends on the accomplishment of an intellectual and educational task. Even more clearly, the development of a permanent high-level technology depends on the solution of certain intellectual problems. These are all part of the information system, and our hope of achieving the present transition without disaster must largely be based on our ability to develop still further the information revolution in which we are engaged. Unfortunately we are not doing well at this; we are not putting our intellectual resources in the field where the problems lie, namely, in the study of social systems; and if war, peace, and population seem such pitfalls today it is largely because we leave these areas to folk culture and do not allow the information revolution to penetrate them. One of the major needs of our time is to devote a massive effort to research in peace, population, and stable high-level technology, and if we delay this too long it may become too late.

In the midst of this enormous transition, and in these centuries which are the most critical in the four-billion-year history of this planet, the Christian will be impelled to ask where stands his own faith. A change as enormous as that through which we are now passing cannot fail to make an impact on every aspect of man's life and thought. We must recognize humbly that the great transition began in a Christian civilization. We may, it is true, trace the origins of science back to the Greeks and the Babylonians, and this torch was handed on mainly through Islam rather than through medieval Christianity. Medieval Christian Europe was, indeed, an obscure peninsula on the edge of the great civilization of Islam. Islam, however, died upon the vine, or perhaps Tamerlane killed it. At any rate it was Europe and its American extension that produced Galileo, Newton, Dalton, Darwin, and Einstein. This, I think, was no accident. Those whose faith is in the Word made flesh are well equipped to initiate and to receive an information revolution. To many this great process of transition which came out of Christian civilization seems likely to supplant not only civilization but the religion out of which it grew. We would certainly expect to find the institutions of Christianity undergoing great sociological modification in the course of a transition in the state of man as profound as that which leads to the abundant society. Sociological transformation, however, is nothing new to Christianity, which has a remarkable ability to take different social forms from, say, the Caesaropapism of Byzantium to the fierce individualism of the Adventist sects. At the core of the Christian faith, however, is not a philosophical doctrine or a scientific theory, but a particular historical event—the resurrection—of unusual symbolic significance. The historical evidence is unlikely to receive much addition, and the symbolic significance is unlikely to be affected by mere affluence, which is powerless before the inescapable necessity of death. I suspect, therefore, that the transition to abundance will not greatly affect the historical and symbolic core of Christianity, much as it may affect its external organization. Furthermore, it may well be that it is only as we move toward the abundant society that the ethic of the New Testament becomes more than a holy ambition for the few; it becomes a necessity for society at large. In the nuclear age we must learn to love our enemies, painful as it is to acquire this skill. The control of population must rest ultimately on a deep personal acceptance of moral responsibility, and the progress of science and technology themselves depends on deep respect for the truth and a high standard of personal integrity.

There are those who disapprove of the abundant society, seeing in it only a universal opportunity for excess, licentiousness, vulgarity, and decadence. We must admit that this indeed could be its shape, and a society of abundance might well be one in which the dignity of mankind is lost. If this were to become true, I am sure that the abundance would not endure. It is a Christian hope, however, that man is capable of heaven even on earth, and that he has within him the potential even to endure bliss.

## 2

# MAN AND SOCIETY IN THE NEW ERA

### by John V. P. Lassoe, Jr.

> At some unmarked point during the past twenty years
> we imperceptibly moved out of the Modern Age and into
> a new, as yet nameless, era. Our view of the world
> changed; we acquired a new perception and with it new
> capacities. There are new frontiers of opportunity, risk
> and challenge. There is a new spiritual center to human
> existence.
>
> PETER DRUCKER, *Landmarks of Tomorrow*

A new era is upon us. That we may have been moving inexorably toward it for over three hundred years need not be argued; neither is there reason to dispute the idea that we have barely begun to taste the fruits, both sweet and bitter, of what some choose to call the "Age of Automation" and of what others hail as the advent of a society of abundance.

The discernible fact is that something is afoot. A few can articulate their impressions or pinpoint the trends, but most of us simply feel it in our bones as a vague excitement or, perhaps more often, as an indefinable sense of oppression. Adlai Stevenson is quoted as saying, "I am glad to have lived at this time";[1] others are not so sure. There is uncertainty, of course, in any time of transition, but this one suggests persistent problems that will mar full enjoyment of whatever lies ahead.

It seems that there will be much to enjoy in the new era. We are all aware of a revolution in technology and in man's productive capacity, and we are told that this revolution has just begun. Improved transportation has given us seven-league boots to circle the earth in a day, and our spacemen are edging ever closer to the moon. Improved communications have given us eyes and ears around the world, and the miracle of television becomes commonplace. Our standard of living advances steadily, and astonishing luxury goods flood the markets—and our homes. Advances in medical science and in public-health practices offer dramatic answers to centuries-old disease riddles, and our life expectancy increases each year. Even the less fortunate benefit from new concepts and services in the field of welfare: no one starves to death in America today. We are on the verge of developing extraordinary new sources of power, and—as Kenneth E. Boulding has observed—this energy revolution, coupled with the dramatic information revolution, could well bring us to the threshold of a society of abundance.

But the other side of the coin has a bleaker hue. We know that we ourselves are part of the increasing mobility of the American people, and we have begun to feel the accompanying rootlessness that bewilders families and demoralizes communities. As masses of people draw ever closer together in a metropolis, we feel the squeeze of mounting urban congestion and suburban crowding. We sense a widening of the gap between the citizen and the seats of power and become uneasily aware that we participate less and less in the determination of our fate and future. We know that we are being depersonalized increasingly by the pressures for conformity that are part and parcel of mass society, and our sense of loneliness is intensified. We are beginning to learn, sometimes painfully, the full meaning of technological unemployment and educational lack. We are becoming acutely conscious of racial tension, and we are disturbed by our feelings of racial hatred or racial guilt. We have more time on our hands than we are able to use happily—and we are told that we are to have even more. Something is happening to our most cherished institution, the family, and we are not quite sure what to do about it. Nuclear annihilation hangs heavily over our heads and we find ourselves asking, "What is the meaning of it all?"

The individual is at the bottom of the heap in this pile-up of social forces and human innovations, and a democratic society has no choice but to find some answers to the problems he poses. There are many Cassandras loose in the land, and some may feel that they have cried their warnings too widely, but the fact remains that man's individuality and dignity are slipping away. Increasing depersonalization seems to negate both real individualism and deep identification with groups, and the process, unchecked, can lead only to collectivism, where man does not count at all. The mission of the Church in the new era seems clear, but the problems are great, and the clock cannot be stopped or turned back. Answers must be sought in the context of a continuing process of social change, for change is the norm in the nameless age that we have entered.


## MASSES AND MIGRATION

There are more and more of us, we are more mobile, and we are crowding together. There are all kinds of staggering statistics, but the simplest one tells us that, at the present birth rate, the number of people in the world will increase from three billion to six billion by the end of this century. A relatively modest projection suggests that the U.S. Census Bureau will count well over three hundred million Americans at that point.

Our new citizens will have to live someplace, and the experts agree that most of them will be in the metropolitan areas. Since the central cities' population is almost stable, we can assume that the bulk of metropolitan growth will occur in the ever widening suburban rings. In any case, America's population —15 per cent urban in 1850, 70 per cent urban today—will be even more overwhelmingly urban by the year 2000.

Migration will be a major factor in this urban growth— a significant part of the continuing flow will be from rural areas where farms, increasingly mechanized, need fewer workers to fill urban mouths. Today, one person can produce enough food and fiber for twenty-five people; the farm population, already down to 12 per cent of the total, is still too high. Over two-thirds of our farm families live in poverty.

There are other reasons for migration, of course. Some move in response to occupational demands made by industry on its junior and middle-level executives; others move to seek new opportunity when traditional urban sources of income and subsistence wither away, as in the "pockets" of unemployment created by technology. The significant fact is that one American in five moves each year, five million of them across state lines and another five million across county lines.

Thus are sown seeds of transiency and rootlessness. Families leave familiar neighborhoods and sever comfortable communal associations to become "newcomers" (often only briefly at that) in strange surroundings. Even the families that stay at home find their roots exposed as friends move away and are replaced by strangers, often of a different racial or ethnic group. If the migrating family loses its sense of stability and community belonging, the changing community loses its sense of cohesiveness and its traditional controls. Needed in the new era are "portable roots" for family and individual—and a new concept of community that will fit shifting populations and increasingly nonresidential patterns of association. This need is demonstrated graphically in urban areas.

## MAN IN METROPOLIS

The city, once defined well by its political boundaries, has all but blended into the sprawling entity that surrounds it. Although only two cities in North America (Miami and Toronto) have accorded full legal recognition to metropolis, no metropolitan area has failed to recognize the economic and social interdependence that binds central city and suburbs together— or the problems in government caused by the multiple political jurisdictions. Even while we are learning to comprehend metropolis and metropolitan planning, we must begin to cope with still another entity of interdependence: megalopolis, such a complex of metropolitan areas as the one that now stretches in almost solid urban and suburban development from Maine to Virginia.

To build metropolis or megalopolis, to house the people and industry and commerce drawn almost irresistibly into its web, we need land. William H. Whyte reports that we are bull-dozing under some three thousand acres of countryside each day, with little heed given to man's need for open space.[2] Save for occasional foresightedness or bold acquisition, we have allowed potential parks and likely recreation areas to be swallowed up indiscriminately until today real countryside is distant from all urbanites and virtually inaccessible for some. The result is a pall of urban grayness over the central city and an unrelieved cluster in its slightly brighter suburbs. This is the physical face of metropolis—fast-changing but, alas, predictable.

The most striking erosion—physically, economically, socially —occurs at the core of metropolis, in the central city, if not downtown (now often the target of dramatic renewal efforts), then in the rings of residence and industry that stretch out to the city line. Here we find the slums inherited by the new-comers to city living, those people least prepared to meet the demands of interdependence imposed by high density. Here we find the deteriorating neighborhoods, the bulk of the sub-standard housing units located in metropolitan areas, the high incidence of crime and poor health and mental illness. Here, in short, we find those left behind in the upward-mobile flight to the suburbs.

"Flight" may be an unfair term for suburbanward move-ment. There is as much pull as push, perhaps more, involved in a family's decision to seek a better life, better housing, better schools and recreation facilities, a little more open space and air; it is unquestionably true that many of these features are to be found in suburban living. But whether frantic flight or reluctant withdrawal, the effect is the same: the city loses its more stable families, much of its potential civic leadership, and an important part of its tax base. Having withdrawn from the city, suburban America continues to look to it for much of its employment, for most of its cultural outlet, for many of its luxury needs, for some of its essential services and, uncon-sciously perhaps, for part of its emotional stimulation. But suburbia is on the outside, looking in only when it chooses;

by and large, it disclaims responsibility for the city and disassociates itself from the city's needs.

All metropolitan citizens share certain sensations, nonetheless, and miracles of mass communication carry many of these facets of urbanism to the three in ten Americans who live in nonurban areas. For one thing, there has been a separation of communal functions: we live in one place, work in another, may play in a third, perhaps shop in a fourth. Family and individual roots, hard enough to sink in a mobile society, become almost unplantable when we cannot identify our real community. Similarly, persons accustomed to the intimate group associations of a small town or unchanging neighborhood, where all needs were met through relatively few memberships, find it hard to draw the same sense of belonging from the network of secondary group associations that characterize communities today. From all this stems the anonymity, the loneliness in a crowd, especially in the anthill of city living, that so many of us feel so often.

## VOICE AND VOTE

The distance between the individual and the nexus of power —be it political, civic, or economic—grows steadily greater, and so does the complexity of issues that a good citizen is expected to understand. Small wonder, then, that the individual feels himself less and less in control over the forces that shape his future. Rightly or wrongly, he translates this feeling of impotence into nonparticipation: it takes a presidential campaign to get out the vote, a strike possibility to bring out union members, and a dramatic local issue to mobilize neighbors. Between crises, those same persons tend to sit at home, overwhelmed by feelings of voicelessness. Scott Greer characterizes the political expectations of both central-city residents and suburbanites (the latter despite their higher average educational and occupational level) as being largely fulfilled by voting and by exercising the "gripe function" in government; only 4 per cent of our voting-age population participates any more fully than that in political affairs.[3]

Participation in society and relationships with the larger community have been mediated in twentieth-century America by a variety of special-interest organizations. As the cities and the nation grew, these voluntary associations multiplied to meet the citizens' need for an organized voice, serving to bridge the widening gap between government and the public, between industry and the worker. The bigness of government and business was matched by a bigness in special-interest groups, and it was possible to mobilize enough pressure to shape official policy in significant areas of life.

But the necessary bigness of voluntary associations has created a new gap, that between members and leadership, and individuals find that they increasingly lack voice and vote in the very groups that they formed to ensure effective participation in political and economic decisions. C. Wright Mills says flatly that "one of the most important of the structural transformations [involved in the transition from public to mass] is the decline of the voluntary associations as a genuine instrument of the public." [4]

## THE CRUSH OF CONFORMITY

These factors combine to make man feel very much alone today. He has become increasingly depersonalized in the bigness of everything around him—big government, big factories, big associations, big cities, big housing developments. The little individual's identity is reduced to digits—a social security number, a military identification number, an account number, an income tax number. If he forgets his name, his number will suffice; if he forgets his number, it may take weeks or months to track down his records. All this flows from the complexity of living; only with such system is order possible.

Man fears aloneness. He wants to be loved and he wants to belong. Erich Fromm calls it man's ceaseless quest for union, a quest that he has most often resolved by choosing the union based on conformity with the group, its customs, practices, and beliefs.[5] Once these were small groups—clan, tribe, settlement, or town—but mass communication has extended the scope of the conforming group to far reaches of the country. The mass media provide daily guidance on the forms and patterns, the current requirements for belonging, that make up the mass culture. The public becomes the mass, and the group member becomes part of mass society.

Mass culture, mass society, then mass control: Peter Drucker warns that "we all but know enough today to turn man into a biological mechanism run by the manipulation of fears and emotions, a being without beliefs, without values, without principles, without compassion, without pride, without humanity altogether." [6] And this can be done, not alone by the threats and terror of totalitarian government, but by the suggestion and persuasion that can be exercised quite comfortably in a democratic society. Here lies another ingredient of the depersonalization that undermines man's individuality.

### JOBS AND AUTOMATION

Technological progress demands new skills, and persons who possess them or who can learn them will enjoy new opportunities for reward in the society of abundance. But the skills will be complex, demanding considerable technical knowledge and an ever higher level of education. The proportion of youth attending high school and college mounts steadily in response to the obvious future demand for professional, technical, and skilled workers. Already 80 per cent of the young people of high-school age attend high school, and 35 per cent of the appropriate age group (nearly 50 per cent in the metropolitan areas) are enrolled in colleges and universities.

But if increased automation and increased productivity reward the skilled and the educated, they hold out little hope for the unskilled and the uneducated. The labor force will grow annually by something like two and a half million workers over the next decade, but the number of unskilled and semi-skilled workers needed by industry will remain constant. Statistical projections are tricky in the era of technological leaps and bounds, but it seems clear that the creation of new jobs will not keep pace with our population increase. Some must lose out in the scramble for work, and it is not hard to predict who the losers will be: older skilled workers, displaced by technological advances, and not yet ready for retirement but considered too old for retraining; unskilled workers past school age, who lack the requisite education for skill-training but find less and less demand for raw labor; and adolescents among the 30 per cent of high school students who drop out before completing their courses and who thus surrender their future before they even start to work. Clearly, education will widen the gap between those who have found a niche in automation's work force and those who find themselves left behind.

Tragically, we already face a situation in which our society has separated itself into two cultures, defined by one writer as "the affluent, educated, productive, and urbanized, those in short who participate in the rich productivity of modern society, on the one hand, and on the other, the poor, uneducated, and unproductive, those who are largely denied the privileges and benefits of which we so often boast." [7] In the metropolitan areas, these two cultures emerge as an affluent suburbia and a deficient central city, three-fourths of the people living in comfort and one-fourth living in poverty.

Poverty and underutilization are not confined to urban areas. National estimates of America's poor vary widely, as do definitions of poverty, but it is a hard fact that somewhere between thirty-eight million and fifty million people—one-fourth of the nation—lack adequate food and housing, education and medical care. They are "maimed in body and spirit, existing at levels beneath those necessary for human decency." [8] Among them are the bulk of the unemployed, the unskilled laborers, the household workers, the farmers and farm laborers. Among them are over two-thirds of our senior citizens. Among them are over half of those with less than four years' high-school education and over 65 per cent of those with less than eight years' elementary education. Among them are over 70 per cent of the people living in substandard housing. [9] There are few signs to suggest that the technological revolution will raise their standard of living through increased employment opportunities—and not many signs that their standard of living will be raised materially. "The poor are always with us"—in the new era, too?

A MATTER OF RACE

There is another characteristic of America's poor: among them are 60 per cent of the Negroes in the United States! Technological unemployment, educational disadvantage, voicelessness, and slum congestion have special meaning for Americans of color. The long history of discrimination and segregation continues to take its toll, even when the doors of opportunity are forced or thrown open. Traditionally the last hired and the first fired, Negro workers are hit hardest when technological displacement occurs, but who is to say that the seniority principle is in itself discriminatory? Education is the key to skill-training and, therefore, to employment in the new era, but when all the racial barriers are swept away in business and industry, who will compensate for the fact that Negroes lag behind whites in years of schooling and in quality of education?

If a growing sense of voicelessness troubles all citizens, there is some comfort to be gained from the right to vote; what then of Negroes in the South who still struggle grimly to exercise the franchise? Affluent America pushes into the suburbs, seeking a better way of life, the pride of home ownership, a little more of a place in the sun; but what of Negro Americans who have education, aspirations, and money to spend—and still may not live in what a former mayor of Philadelphia called the "white noose" around our cities? One does not have to be unskilled or uneducated to be left behind in the Age of Automation; one need simply be a Negro.

Significantly, the rising tide of expectations that characterizes the new era has not passed the Negro by. A growing impatience with civil-rights lag—the failure of equal opportunity in practice to keep pace with equal opportunity in law—has expressed itself in accelerated efforts to challenge discrimination on all fronts. But there is more to this than heightened activity alone: there is also a growing sense of racial pride and racial consciousness, sparked in no small measure by the leap to freedom of the old African colonies and by the rising influence of colored people in world affairs. A few Negroes have translated this into a new racism, the "black nationalism" of such groups as the Black Muslims, but the more important implications lie elsewhere.

Leadership in the civil-rights movement has passed from the hands of sympathetic whites into those of Negroes, who now provide its direction and set its pace. Many other factors are at work: increased political power, particularly in large northern cities but increasingly in the South; increased economic power, now being wielded in boycotts and selective-buying campaigns; increased levels of education and civic sophistication; increased intervention by government at all levels; the impact of American race relations on our image abroad. But the salient point is that Negro Americans, tired of waiting for the dominant majority to decide that the time is ripe for full enjoyment of rights already guaranteed by law, have taken the initiative in a drive for full citizenship.

The mood of the "new Negro" is such that compromise is no longer possible; delay is no longer being accepted passively. Social change does not occur without tension, and racial tension will continue until there is racial equality. Because human feelings are involved, elements of racial antagonism, guilt, resentment, even hatred, will be found in that tension. And because groups are made up of individuals, it is the individual —white and Negro alike—who will experience those feelings, adding to his over-all uneasiness in the new era.

## THE NEW LEISURE: TREAT OR THREAT

It is abundantly clear that technological progress will make it possible for us to produce more in less time and with less physical effort, and that we will be freed increasingly from much of the time once spent in working. Brawn will give way to brain in the Age of Automation, and nonwork will replace work as the major time block in our lives.

Work provides us with meaning. It is the central fact around which we organize our lives and usually, despite the disclaimer that we have to work in order to earn a living, it is our prime outlet for self-expression and our major opportunity to experience feelings of self-fulfillment. Technological advances—the assembly line among them—are robbing our work of much of its identification with individual effort and its elements of creative pride, but even more depersonalization lies ahead. As this gap between the worker and the end product of his work widens, what new opportunities for meaning and achievement will he find?

Beyond this, we face a change in our view of the nature of work. Because work was considered more important than play, we have taken most seriously the work that looked least like play, the more obviously physical or physically productive work. But the work of knowledge is becoming the specifically productive work, and the man who works exclusively or primarily with his hands is the one who is increasingly unproductive. If we continue to look to work for meaning, we must reckon with its changing nature, too.

Perhaps we will do better to look for meaning in the growing nonwork area of our lives. Shorter work days, shorter work

weeks, and shorter working lives seem to be our lot, and some
persons seem destined to face the fact of no work at all. It is
not too early to face the consequences of a utopian existence
in which people will earn their living by a minimum of effort—
and in which they will face the knotty problem of how to get
through the day. In the past, society has claimed that its members were entitled to a living only if they carried out a task
defined by society as valuable and for which it was willing to
pay. In the society of abundance, on the other hand, people
will be able to follow an interest they find vital, but which
society will not support through the price mechanism. There
will be a clinging identification of "useful" to work that has
economically productive ends, but enlightened arrangements
may help to give a definition to nonproductive work that will
remove it from the category of leisure—and save it from the
fate described by Margaret Mead:

> Now, in our eyes, leisure is very dangerous. In this country, we
> are all—regardless of our denominational positions—inheritors of
> the Puritan ethic, and we believe that the difference between virtue
> and vice is at what time the pain comes. If the pain comes first and
> the pleasure afterwards—that is virtue. This attitude governs every-
> thing we do: if we work hard enough, we are entitled to a little
> leisure. Leisure is rest, and no one is entitled to rest who has not
> first worked.[10]

## THE AMERICAN FAMILY

The American worker tends to spend his nonwork hours with
his family. But even family seems to fail the individual. For one
thing, the family is no longer a closely knit unit to which the
individual belongs, but merely part of a wider social environment to which he earlier becomes attentive. Transiency, tech-

nology, and conformity have played their parts in reshaping the family as the basic social unit. The concept of family has narrowed. Clans or extended kinship groups have disappeared; uncles, aunts, cousins, brothers, and sisters are scattered across the country, out of touch and seldom seen. Even grandparents become more remote. Population statistics may show proportionately more young children and more senior citizens in our ranks, but they see less and less of each other as the two-generation home becomes the rule. Family comes to mean father, mother, and children—with only peripheral or occasional contact with other relatives.

There are many reasons for the new concept of family, and the lessening of family interdependence is a significant one. The family, once a producing unit that needed all the manpower it could muster to stay alive, is now a consuming unit in which one breadwinner (or, increasingly, two breadwinners) must provide for all other mouths. Children and aging relatives become economic liabilities, not assets, especially with the high cost of new housing and the fact of families on the move.

There is another aspect of the lessening of family interdependence. Families that worked together played together and stayed together; now, father, mother, and children are apart most hours of the day, each living in a circle of associations and experiences that seldom touches those of the other members. Whether increased time away from work will develop new patterns of leisure interdependence in the family unit remains to be seen.

Individuals find role confusion in the family, too. Erich Fromm observes that equality once meant, in a religious context, that we were all God's children, that we were all one, but that each one of us was a unique entity, a cosmos by itself, and that the very differences between us must be respected. But today, he holds, equality means sameness and, in terms of the family, equality is bought at this price: women are equal because they are not different any more. Men and women become the same, not equals at opposite poles. In the trend toward "teamship" in marriage and "togetherness" in family, there is a blurring of role and function. Husband and wife wash dishes together and go off to work together, and it becomes that much harder to preserve the subtle difference between equality and sameness. Parents and children share in family decision-making, and it becomes that much harder to differentiate between occasions for democratic participation and occasions for exercise of legitimate parental control.[11]

Working women are on the increase: more than one-third of the women of working age in the United States are employed or are actively seeking employment, compared with less than one-fifth in 1890. Significantly, the proportion of those who are married and have children has risen sharply. Technology has made this possible by creating more jobs that can employ women, more jobs where brains and dexterity take priority over brawn. Technology and other factors have also exerted a pushing force by easing the burden of homemaking, by stimulating the demand for desirable but nonessential goods that an extra income can purchase for the family, and by helping to create the boredom and lack of fulfillment at home that drive some women to seek work.

Discussion of technology and the family must give heed to a phenomenon first observed during the Great Depression and noted increasingly by students of technological displacement: the emasculation of men who, thrust out of work and forced into the ranks of the permanently unemployed, become dependent on welfare or on the income of other members of the family, losing in the process the self-respect and sense of fulfillment that came from their function as breadwinner. Sadly, men at nonwork are multiplying.

## THE MEANING OF IT ALL

"Even the future isn't what it used to be." The future must now be contemplated under the sobering possibility of nuclear annihilation. We may yet improve on existing weapons, but we cannot achieve means of destruction more total than those already available. Man has lived with fear before as he faced war and death and life, but the dimensions of this threat are different. There is no place to hide, except in madness and, significantly, the incidence of mental illness is rising.

Our sense of immortality, however false, has been threatened. Building for the future of one's family becomes somewhat less satisfying when the future is so uncertain. Mobility has not helped: the building or buying of the family home, in which people then expected to live until death, was an important part of our future not too many years ago. The home that was acquired, the roots that were sunk in the community, and the network of friends and neighbors that was developed were all part of the heritage that we felt we were leaving to our children. Now, none of these is ours to leave.

The devaluation of traditional principles, finally, gives man the feeling that the world he is leaving behind is not only different ("Things just aren't the same any more"), but somehow worse. If the future is uncertain, his value judgments must be made on the basis of the present. He sees that the transiency and rootlessness have spawned *anomie*, a normlessness reflected

in declining standards of moral conduct. He sees that depersonalization at work, at play, in the community is eroding individuality and differentiation. He knows that the quickened pace
of living and the overstimulation of the senses have robbed
life of many of its pleasures, "the things I used to enjoy when
I was young." Small wonder then that he asks himself in the
dark of night, "Why bother?"

**3**

# SOCIAL ETHIC IN THE NEW ERA

## by Kenneth Underwood

A new generation is coming to power in America—in business, politics, education, the churches. It is forging its own responses to a changing world, as past generations have done. Those of us concerned with the morality and religion of a nation need to be sensitive to these new moods and ways of thought and action. Otherwise, we may in our concern to prove the continuity and validity of the age-old doctrines of our faith—that men are sinful, finite, dependent upon the grace of God— ignore the unique expressions of God's work in the world and the new patterns of values and personal involvement in response.

I am here going to confine my observations to one segment of American leadership, those who are now in mid-career in the large business corporations, for they are perhaps the most self-conscious representatives of a shift in social ethics that is taking place on the American scene.

The major characteristics of the new social ethic now emerging among sentinel figures in the business community are these: first, an awareness of new moral choices made possible by technological and scientific advances, of alternatives of action not open to leaders of past generations; second, a broadening and deepening of their involvement in significant associations in American society, accompanied by an enhancement of personal identity and reality; third, a rejection of ideological, one-dimensional approaches to problems in favor of multifactored approaches.

## CHOICES THAT ARE MORALLY SIGNIFICANT

The papers given at the American Marketing Association meeting in December, 1961, were mainly directed to an appraisal of the new choices confronting businessmen, given the impact of technology and science upon the society. For example, the American people now have a greater opportunity than ever before to exercise individual interests and values in their decisions as to where they will work and what they will purchase. In earlier periods capital was limited, and the automatic technical devices for liberating men from the most repetitive and physically burdensome work were not available. Also, the whole legal, political, and economic setting enforced much more rigorous organizational control over individuals. Today, however, the social and economic controls of business, which made possible the "chewing up" of millions of immigrant people in the establishment of a modern, continental nation, simply are no longer sanctioned in most communities. And the technical resources for alternative treatment of persons are now available.

Business leaders rightly regard this fact as of profound moral significance. The technical accomplishment itself is not to be viewed as the product of automatons, but of persons with the self-discipline, imagination, and humility necesary to shape and to be shaped by modern industrial and commercial organization. New patterns of authority are emerging to integrate the goals of individuals and of enterprise as a whole, to expand the roles of men in their work, and to express motivations other than economic gain.

The technical expansion of man's power to control nature and society surely must have significance in God's purpose for men. For the first time in history man now has the ability to subdue the earth, to use it for human purposes throughout the world, to organize institutions so that the wealth and knowl-edge of one nation can be a determining factor in the eradica-tion of the poverty, mass disease, and illiteracy of another nation.

To stress this aspect of our new moral occasion is not to ignore the fact that crucial spiritual battles still go on in the souls of men as to what are to be the standards of good to direct the use of these powers. The opportunities for greater freedom and diversity of choice, for beauty in functional design, for careers in business that do not produce trivia will go unseized if men do not aspire to make of their lives something more than pursuit of the fast buck. But the opportunities for the realization of personal potentialities and powers are present in our time as never before.

## A NEW INVOLVEMENT

The second aspect of the new social ethic is the self-conscious and critical way in which business leaders are increasingly moving in and out of a whole network of associations and roles in society. This stands in sharp contrast to previous generations of businessmen who either sought to avoid involvement in organizations that took their attention from business or tried to "operate" in the universities, churches, politics, mass media, etc., as if these were simply an extension of their business careers.

Many businessmen work closely with several associations of cultural and economic significance. They try not to act in them as if they were instruments of business; they go to great lengths (I have studied closely men in a number of these associations) to understand the internal dynamics and distinctive purposes of such institutions as the liberal arts college, the policy-research group, the party organizations, etc. While they often begin with presuppositions quite distinct from those that determine the association's work, they do not neatly resolve these tensions by applying a business-interest formula.

### LEARNING EXPERIENCES

These men are aware that things need to be done and said in politics, in the university, in the church, etc., that cannot be done and said in business. Indeed, this is what attracts them and stimulates them. As one business executive remarked: "After a certain rung of the ladder has been reached in business, we have all the money we really need, we have won the respect of our business associates, we do our work effectively. From here on out, we are looking for activities with certain risks involved, with new problems, with a chance for greatness, or at least for making a contribution to society that is different than business itself can make."

College presidents and faculty treat these men less and less as if they were merely status seekers to be flattered into fund-raising. Rather, the academic community recognizes their desire to be involved in genuine learning experiences. Suburban pastors, too, are discovering that some of their key business leaders are worrying less about new church buildings and more about the quality of the study, discussion, and worship that go on inside of them.

The sentinel figures I am describing do not fit well the models dear to the popular sociologist and moralist, either of autonomous men trying to find personal identity by "bucking the organization" or of men who take "the vows" of conformity to the mores of business. Their personal being is more basic than their social functions, but their personal existence requires their involvement in shaping highly technical organizations to meet the genuine needs of people and in relating these organizations in such a mutual and complementary way as to achieve a viable society. They are trying to articulate a social ethic that appreciates the depths of personal accountability and the social conditions making possible significant choice and action.

Perhaps what is slowly and painfully emerging in America is a post-technical society in which more and more people cross the threshold of fragmented existence (playing out unrelated roles in business, politics, church, family) or of monopolized existence (simply the agents of a particular institution) to a new mode of relating themselves to society.

The men I have talked with and studied are trying to discern what the future society may be, could be, with the giving of their own commitment and substance to it. They believe they are utterly realistic as to their social situation and the realizable programs or developments within it. Descriptive and normative modes of analysis interpenetrate in their thinking. They sense a gap between their achievement and the possibilities of the associations over which they have some influence.

## FROM "PRINCIPLE" TO COMMITMENT

The thinking of the businessmen I am describing is not ideological, abstract, or wholistic. This is the third characteristic
of the new social ethic. Their thought does not move from some
general "proposition" or ideological "principle" about the
shape of the whole society or its fundamental assumptions
about man, down to the particular. Rather it moves out from
the technical problems and the feel for them developed in an
organization to the larger forces and ideas that operate in the
problem. Businessmen are increasingly accustomed to thinking
in terms of concrete choices they can make, breaking down the
different aspects of society into manageable objects for human
understanding and action.

The vice president of a large management consultation firm
recently explained this aspect of the "new" and the "old"
social ethic. A prep school's board of trustees was considering
whether it would actively support efforts to secure federal funds
for their school, thus reducing for parents and private donors
the burden of rising educational costs. An elderly insurance
company president opposed such a move "on the clear basis
that the school stood for the principle of freedom of education
from governmental control."

The younger vice president objected; he argued that a
"decision on the matter must be a responsible one but could
not be made on the basis of such a single principle. The board
must consider the situation in terms of the rising costs of
education, the extent to which safeguards against governmental control could be assured, the over-all balance the school
might maintain between various sources of funds, the kind
of educational programs the school wished to undertake, etc."

The new social ethic represented here sees responsibility in terms of the health and growth of a corporate enterprise and the fulfillment of its just and necessary functions in the society, rather than in allegiance to a particular principle. In religious terms, I would see this social ethic asserting that the trustees of an institution are called to obedience to God, not to a particular norm such as freedom from the government. Obedience to God in the concrete situation (e.g., in deciding on the policy of a school) is the act required, not the punctilious practice of a particular virtue. No business, school, or any other institution was ever maintained out of freedom or love alone, but only out of the engagement and commitment of the full resources of men. This conviction is the basis of opposition to ideological ethics of the past.

These, then, are the three major characteristics of the new social ethic. The question is how widely and deeply its proponents' attitude and approach to moral problems can permeate the atmosphere and structure of business.

### CRACKING THE BARRIER

The battles now being waged over the content of political education programs carried on by corporations are a case in point. These programs involve most of the major corporations and trade associations in the United States and thousands of managerial and supervisory personnel. Let us grant that the programs of the past three or four years represent a gain over the more crass and partisan efforts of earlier years. Still they are remarkably alike in their basic assumption that the interests of business and of the public are the same, and in their concentration on techniques of organizing campaigns and winning elections to the exclusion of substantive issues. And many of the memoranda submitted to superiors by executives in charge of these programs assume agreement among businessmen on the "more favorable environment" wanted from politics and take for granted that all businessmen are going to find their way into the same grand old party.

These political education courses grow out of and reinforce the illusion that business executives have become so enlightened as to the needs of others, the corporations' interests so vast and complex, their demands so restrained that business is now able to assume that what is good for it is good for America and vice versa. What this version of the "social responsibility" image ignores—and what I noted was being grasped with increasing realism by the sentinel figures in business—is the fact that politics has its own life and demands, which are not to be equated with those of other institutions.

Unfortunately the literature on "practical politics" used by business rarely mentions, let alone highlights or explores, any of the social, moral, and religious reasons for the democratic political process—a process in which genuine conflict, as well as accord, between private and public goals is recognized as a fact of life. In this process—when it works well—no group is able to dominate the government for long or to keep others from influencing it. The public good is defined in policy by leaders who are responsible to an electorate and are supported by competing parties accommodating to a variety of interests.

## A FREIGHTED QUESTION

An additional fact to note about this political literature is that it does not reflect the realities that emerge in the discussions of the courses, even when taught "by the book." Those businessmen who have experienced politics at first hand and who draw upon interpretations of their college courses know the necessary compromises that frustrate the ideologist and the business careerist alike. Thus the question, what are the grounds of one's involvement in society, the resources by which defeat, tragedy, disillusionment are to be faced? cannot be evaded in the education of public leaders.

The most pervasive and emotionally freighted question in social ethics for business is the relation of government to the whole range of private associations in society. For this new generation of leaders the problem is not to be solved simply on the principles of the past, but out of deep involvement in the responsibilities of the present and the possibilities of the future. If one asks whether their social ethic is entirely pragmatic and circumstantial, the reply is: "We are men of principle, the principle being that of acceptance of full responsibility as persons for the health and growth of institutions in our care."

This may in the future lead to all kinds of partnerships or mutual arrangements between government and private associations, even though these were once thought to be destructive of creativity and freedom. But it will also mean greater rigor and precision in business thought as to what are the distinctive and what are the shared functions and values of various organizations in the society. For most of these men the criteria for judgment in relation to specific programs are confused and contradictory. Still to be worked out, for instance, are the relations of the federal government, business, churches, schools in support of efforts by underdeveloped societies to realize the gains of modern technology.

## "WHOLE MEN"

One thing is certain, however. The men who act in the world seek to be whole men—not businessmen or churchmen—with a self-consciousness and drive not present for decades. The men described here—if they are Christians—make no claim to have reached some level of altruism or sinlessness not achieved by other generations. They claim only that they are confronted with new choices made possible by advances in man's power to communicate, to control nature, to fashion social organizations, and they believe that men who live in the faith, love and hope of the gospel cannot regard these choices as insignificant. Through them will be expressed the faith in a God who uses the work of each generation for his purposes; the love of God that directs the use of factories, mass media, political controversy in the service of men at home and abroad; the hope in an eternal life that makes their acts in business and public life bearable and negotiable in their relativity.

These men want study and discussion in the Church that has the rigor and quality they experience elsewhere. They want it directed to their loneliness, their loss of courage to act, their fuzziness about how their varied roles are to be meaningfully related, their guilt and remorse over the hurt and suffering they inflict, the truth they keep from others, the elite snobbery they develop in the process of producing their "most important product—progress." To date few pastors have been able to fashion settings in the Church where men see and hear the phenomena I have described, let alone provide dialogue with business and public leaders that draws meaningfully upon the traditional images of the gospel.

The grounds of the action now needed in our world will

not be found in the traditional American ethic of self-fulfillment measured by material reward, but by creativity in sacrifice
that is grasped only by the most profound moral and religious
commitment.

## 4

# THE MISSION OF THE CHURCH IN THE NEW ERA

### by Arthur E. Walmsley

I

Historians of the future will probably consider our generation as the one in which Christendom came to an end. By "Christendom" is meant the close identification of the Christian religion with the political, social, and economic structures of Western society. Since the acceptance of Christianity by Constantine in the fourth century, some form of accommodation between Church and society has prevailed in the West, both as the basis of public institutions and as a formal standard of private morality. Christianity clearly was understood to be the religion of the West. To the extent that the West dominated the life of the world, the Christian religion had an influence, by no means all for the good, far beyond the numbers of its practicing adherents. Today, the marriage of Church and society is fast dissolving, brought on by the growing secularization of the West itself, and by the challenge to Western hegemony put by the peoples of Africa, Asia, and Latin America, not only in political and economic affairs, but in the realm of ideology. The process has moved so far as to render the concept of

58

"Christendom" obsolete. Christendom as a fact no longer exists. Yet Church leadership, notably in North America, continues to act as if Christian faith and life were central to our public and private order. We are, as one critic put it, a minority with a majority complex.

It is not, after all, easy to unlearn sixteen hundred years of experience. The Constantinian settlement changed the Church from a radical sect within the empire to its dominant and frequently ruthless ideology, and opened the way for the creation of Christendom. The medieval synthesis came to represent a high mark in the accommodation of Church and society. Church and state were largely coterminous. The local parish was at once an ecclesiastical, political, economic, and sociological unit. A theology of society, of the market place, of law and justice was woven into the fabric of Western Christian civilization. The flowering of this culture did not die easily. It is true, as R. H. Tawney, Ernst Troeltsch, Max Weber, and others have catalogued, that the rise of capitalism, the emergence of the national state, and the Reformation shattered the unity of the medieval synthesis. The Christian religion was bent to new patterns of economic life and emerging nationalism, and the institutional church ceased to exercise a hold on guild organization, just-price theory, and other aspects of community life. Scholasticism gave way to a cultural and philosophical fascination with the ancient world. The organic unity of the Church was shattered. Theology was deposed as queen of the sciences. But the active partnership of the Church with Western civilization continued, albeit that Protestant and Catholic both invoked Christ as a kind of household god in the endless wars of religion. The colonial experiment saw friars marching with conquistadors, and missionaries under the banner of Victoria Regina. The explosion of Christian missions in the nineteenth and early twentieth centuries was almost unparalleled in Church history, even as it paralleled the economic exploitation of colonial peoples. The rise to power of the greatest "Christian" nation of the modern era, the United States, led to the easy assurance, practically unchallenged until World War II, that the primacy of Christianity in the religious life of the world would prevail.

The price paid by the Church during its accommodation to the modern world has been its successive withdrawal from human affairs, and the growth of an autonomous secular order. It was a major step from the medieval concept of the just price to the religious individualism of the Protestant ethic. It is but one step further to a science of "pure" economics. Politics, even of warring princes, was closely woven into the theology and practice of the Middle Ages. Religious wars in the period of the Enlightenment fractured the unity of a Holy Roman Empire by asserting a divine right of princes and opened the door to a rationale of democracy grounded not in God but in the rights of man, resulting ultimately in the establishment of the modern secular state. The nineteenth-century battle between science and religion was alternately won and lost by religion, *won* in the sense that Christian writers in the end accepted the new knowledge as coming from God, *lost* in the more fundamental sense that science continued to develop into a highly complex system, or indeed many systems, of analysis, completely autonomous of theological considerations. Institutional religion emptied itself of direct confrontation of the secular order, and became immersed in "religion," a religiosity as separate and autonomous from the totality of life as each of the emerging specializations of the modern era.

On the whole, the West has not as yet found it necessary to unseat the Church from an institutional place in the society (although attempts have been made, as in France after the first revolution or as in Mexico earlier in this century). The Church has, on its part, accepted an increasingly peripheral position with regard to the dominant economic, political, social, and intellectual issues of the age. How far this has proceeded may be seen by the readiness churchmen display to accept purely ceremonial functions in public life, as in the embarrassingly meaningless recitation of invocations at public events (always on a careful formula respecting the "three-faith" structure of formal religion, or "four-faith" if the Orthodox are not overlooked) and the public horror displayed by some churchmen over Supreme Court decisions barring trivial religious exercises in otherwise secular schools.

## II

We have moved into a new era. Its economic landscape, and the colossal adjustments demanded of men who live in this new world, are the concerns of this volume. That it is fast wiping away the familiar patterns of thought, community life, and social organization of the Protestant ethic should be readily observable. Professor Kenneth E. Boulding has sketched the emergence of a society dominated by advanced forms of industrial production, by the impact of scientific exploration and automation. Mr. John V. P. Lassoe, Jr., has suggested some of the human and social problems created by urbanization, and by the social engineering which accompanies urban-industrial growth. Dr. Kenneth Underwood touches on the new problems of ethics created by corporate decision-making in advanced industrial society. The new social structures of our era are largely untouched by the Church. Yet they are the principalities and powers, the vast worlds within which men live, work, and make the choices that affect the destiny of millions as of themselves. These new powers, as Bishop E. R. Wickham observes, exercise "an influence beyond that of the 'flesh and blood' administering them. They both create and express the 'feel' of the nation, form its public philosophy, colour society, create its 'angelic' or 'demonic' character, and can hold 'flesh and blood' as prey. This is not exaggeration, and the monolithic, totalitarian State is but an extreme expression of it." [1]

In the growth of two areas, corporate power and government, the fact of power is most readily apparent. Technology has placed within reach of the whole human family the power to solve the basic human needs of food, shelter, and a minimum standard of living. But modern technology cannot exist without the mobilization of the energies of countless persons. Centralized planning is an inescapable dimension of the new era. A. A. Berle, Jr., points out, for example, that about 50 per cent of American manufacturing is held by about 150 corporations.

If a rather large group is taken, the statistics would probably show that about two-thirds of the economically productive assets of the United States, excluding agriculture, are owned by a group of not more than 500 corporations. This is actual asset ownership. . . . But in terms of power, without regard to asset positions, not only do 500 corporations control two-thirds of the non-farm economy but within each of that 500 a still smaller group has the ultimate decision-making power. This is, I think, the highest concentration of power over economics which makes the medieval feudal system look like a Sunday School party.[2]

Side by side with the growth of corporate power, the twentieth century has seen the emergence of big government. In the established nations of the West, government has come to assume an increasingly central role in the regulation of massive economic power; in addition, it has stepped in to support education, human welfare, and other aspects of domestic life, the problems of which outstrip the abilities of the voluntary sector (and the churches) to solve. Government in the emerging nations of Africa, Latin America, and Asia has, from the beginning of independence in those areas, not only assumed responsibility for the total welfare of the people, but rapidly displaced church and other voluntary programs of education and welfare, in some cases through confiscation or other forcible means. The ascendancy of government in providing services to the citizenry at the climactic periods of life—birth, nurture, employment, family life, sickness, and death—is as significant as the domination of the society and the individual by large-scale economic enterprise. The Church is almost wholly detached from these massive concentrations of power, both corporate and governmental. These are the dominant realities of contemporary social life, and their very existence undercuts completely traditional understandings of the relation of Church and culture.

The challenge is most apparent in the new countries of Africa and Asia. Christian missions have, in many of these nations, played a commanding role in the provision of welfare and education. With an assertive nationalism, and renascent Islam, Buddhism, or Hinduism a fact in many places, Christian missions are today confronted with hostile or obstructionist governments, or at least ones determined to build "neutral" societies. In its studies of the "Christian responsibility toward areas of rapid social change," the World Council of Churches recognized the tactical necessity in these places of adapting to a nationalistic religious neutrality: "It is the duty of Christians, in co-operation with other citizens, to build a neutral state." [3] And in 1959, a study conference called by the World Council reaffirmed the position: "In the countries of rapid social change . . . there is some measure of religious pluralism and large portions of the population have been secularized. In these countries Christians should work for the development of a state which is neutral as between the various religions represented in it." [4]

Separation of Church and state or, to be accurate, of organized religion and government, is not a new idea to North Americans. Nor is its advocacy by the World Council likely to come as a surprise. There is growing evidence that the Roman Catholic hierarchy, faced with the same problems as their Protestant brethren, are likewise beginning to challenge the traditional understandings of Church and state which have been held in Rome since the fourth century. In 1961, a statement of the Sixth Plenary Assembly of the Episcopate of the Congo went so far as to "recognize the *autonomy* of the State on the political, economic, and social level" (italics added). Msgr. Lorenz Jager, Archbishop of Paderborn, questioned the applicability of traditional Church-state ideas in a speech on January 1, 1960:

From the situation characterizing the times of Constantine—the union of Church and State—we have now arrived at a "distinction" which in certain countries is of a friendly nature; in many other countries, it is neutral; in the majority, outright hostile. Many states seek to destroy every word of Christian culture, or to substitute it with other ideologies. The entering of the colored races into world history, the rebirth of the great non-Christian world religions such as Hinduism and Islam, have created a totally new and different situation in the world, which confronts the Church with new and very difficult tasks. [5]

There are hard facts behind these appraisals of the Church's mission in neutral or hostile cultures. Christians today number about one-third of the world's population. By the year 2000, on the basis of the worldwide population explosion and with the rate of missionary outreach slowed to a halt in many places, the percentage will have dropped to about one in six. It can no longer be assumed that our traditional claims will find a ready ear among "men benighted" who call "us to deliver their land from error's chain." Christianity's long identification with the West is as much a millstone in the new age as it was a point of favor in earlier eras.

The dilemma is not limited to the emerging nations, or to areas of outright persecution as in some of the Iron Curtain countries, South Africa, or the Poruguese colonies. The Christian in America or Western Europe has become increasingly frustrated by the accommodation the Church has made to the modern industrial world. He is well aware of the ways in which contemporary intellectual and cultural values conflict with and undermine Christian belief, but he is largely helpless to know how to make the gospel come alive to the new era. He is dimly aware of the principalities and powers—massive technology, big government, sprawling cities, packaged news. He talks about "penetrating the power structures," but aside from a few experiments here and there the talk about the ministry of the laity in daily work is largely an aspiration and seldom a disciplined effort.

Nowhere is the problem more apparent than in the education of the young. The intensity of the current Church-state debate is a barometer of the feelings of uprootedness American Christians have with respect to their society. The various solutions offered to the current debate on public schools and government aid curiously affirm the same fact: that we are no longer, in any meaningful sense, a Christian nation. A small minority rebel entirely, and urge such meaningless actions as constitutional amendments which would affirm that we are a "Christian nation" in spite of our obvious pluralism. Thoughtful observers such as Bishop James A. Pike advocate a curriculum in the public schools which is "positive" toward the Judeo-Christian heritage. This, it is argued, is consistent with the no-establishment clause of the First Amendment. Perhaps it is. The fact remains that present public education is pervasively secular, and it is doubtful whether any injection of Christian or "Judeo-Christian" substance into the curriculum would be possible on a large-scale basis, or particularly productive if it were. The current posture of the Roman Catholic Church and some Protestants, in favor of some form of financial succor to those who support separate school systems, parallels the reasoning of those who are proponents of a completely neutral public school system; the positions agree on the secularism of public education, and differ only with respect to whether concessions should be made to a religious minority. The debate is a painful and divisive one in American public life. It is unfortunate that there is not greater awareness that the struggle to define what the First Amendment means by no "establishment of religion" is only symbolic of a more fundamental question: How shall the Christian minority adjust to the prevailing secularism of the culture? Whatever the slogans used, the United States, as is true of the West generally, is a secular society and each of the positions affirmed in its own way confirms the fact. The Church-state debate is, to a considerable degree, a holding action during which a new accommodation can be brought about by the Christian minority as it surrenders whatever vestige of Christian "hold" it may have upon the society.

Denis Munby offers a definition of a secular society which fits the American situation today:

"A secular society is one which explicitly refuses to commit itself as a whole to any particular view of the nature of the universe and the place of man in it. The State neither requires subscription to any particular doctrines nor overt forms of religious behavior as a condition for claiming full rights as a citizen; furthermore, it does not in any significant sense attach itself to any church or religion. . . . We need to distinguish between a secular society and State. Society is wider than the State and its operations—even today. A Christian society could indeed exist with a secular State which did not express Christian beliefs in any organized way. But today we have certainly not got a Christian society. In effect, for most important purposes we are a secular society, where it makes little or no difference in what our religion or morality consists, and in which Christians are a small minority. That the State machinery continues to incorporate archaeological fragments appropriate to former periods when society was Christian is of less importance than the dominant mores of society." [6]

### III

The churches of the United States and Europe can recover a sense of mission and ministry only within a recognition of their real predicament. Perhaps the dictum of Dietrich Bonhoeffer is an overstatement: "we are proceeding towards a time of no religion at all; men as they now are simply cannot be religious any more." The facts are that the principalities and powers of the age—political, economic, and social—are largely untouched by the Church, her ordained ministry or, most significantly, by those relatively self-conscious Christians who function within the structures of society. Surely the evidence is overwhelming that the Church must die to its illusions about its place in society, an inherited pattern of some sixteen centuries of uneasy marriage with the culture, if renewal is to take place among the faithful, and Christ's Body is to be discerned where it first was broken, in the world itself.

In God's purpose, the technological revolution holds promise of a new era in human life. From a biblical viewpoint God makes himself known in the facts of history. The almost unlimited possibilities of material abundance together with the opportunities of human encounter and cultural exchange which have been unleashed already have changed human society; more has happened to man's social order in one generation than in all of past history. This process derives of God. Yet the problems it creates for Christian theology are monumental. Three in particular are worth noting at some length:

1. *The relation of power to human values.* As Romano Guardini has observed,

In the coming epoch, the essential problem will no longer be that of increasing power—though power will continue to increase at an ever swifter tempo—but of curbing it. The core of the new epoch's intellectual task will be to integrate power into life in such a way that man can employ power without forfeiting his humanity. For he will have only two choices: to match the greatness of his power with the strength of his humanity, or to surrender his humanity to power and perish. The very fact that we can define these alternatives without seeming utopian or moralistic—because by so doing we but voice something of which the public is more or less aware—is a further indication that the new epoch is overtaking the old.[7]

The Christian doctrine of power is grounded in the doctrine of creation. Man lives in a universe of energy which derives in the first instance from the creative outpouring of God's activity. Within the physical universe, the manipulation of creative energy—man's relation to the natural order—and the ordering of human and social energy—man's relation to his fellows— are the moral issues with which man must come to terms in every era. But as we have already seen, in the new era decision-making takes place increasingly within the context of ever larger structures: the modern corporation, the automated industry, the welfare state—group settings in which decision-making by teams or task forces reduces individual accountability to a minimum.

How is power to be exercised responsibly in this setting? Traditional approaches of personal accountability, as expressed in the Protestant ethic, fail to come to grips with the nature of structure and context of the new era. J. Irwin Miller, leading industrialist and president of the National Council of Churches, cites a problem typical of those which must be faced by Christians if they are to be responsive to the predicament of men in our day:

All persons engaged in economic life are involved . . . in the business of making choices. In my experience, such choices are not too often choices between a clear right and a clear wrong. Most choices, and these are the difficult ones, present themselves as choices between two wrongs; either way you go someone is done an injustice. Let us take the morality of a lay-off, for example, or of an individual discharge. No matter how you decide, someone is truly damaged, most often unfairly.[8]

The humanization of the social order does not reduce itself, in situations such as this, to the categories of Christian love. Social control, the balance of the rights and responsibilities of one group against those of another, involves issues of justice. One cannot withdraw from making decisions about the use of power without rejecting the structure of the world itself, without in fact denying the world which God has made.

Justice seen in this light is not a crude approximation of love, but the means by which the Christian co-operates with the will of God precisely in the midst of life. As William Temple observed,

Associations cannot love one another; a trade union cannot love an employers' federation, nor can one national State love another. The members of one may love the members of the other so far as opportunities of intercourse allow. That will help in negotiations; but it will not solve the problem of the relationships between the two groups. Consequently, the relevance of Christianity in these spheres is quite different from what many Christians suppose it to be. Christian charity manifests itself in the temporal order as a supernatural discernment of, and adhesion to, justice in relation to the equilibrium of power.[9]

The preoccupation of the Church in the postwar world with the dynamics of face-to-face groups reflects a nostalgia, felt by all men confronted by the rapidity of social change, for a simpler society in which personal choice and personal accountability are paramount. But this very genuine effort to "humanize" complex technological society and to bring men to a sense of personal worth has been made in large measure by ignoring the public and economic sectors of life in which the major decisions affecting the future of humankind are being made. It is a major task of the Church to devise the means for engaging the structures of the modern world. For either massive power will be humanized, that is, made susceptible to structures of justice, or man as we know him will perish.[10]

2. *The nature of ministry in the age of abundance.* In seeking to understand how the Church can penetrate the structures of the new society, a considerable examination is going on throughout the Christian world regarding the nature of Christian ministry. The recovery of the ministry of lay people is perhaps the most significant theological breakthrough of the postwar period. But pioneer experiments and generalized treatments about the "scattered Church" are not enough. Significantly, the most fruitful results of vocational conferences have taken place within those professions (law, medicine, the arts) in which a high degree of personal initiative and autonomy are prevalent. *How* the Christian layman exercises his vocation in a massive corporate structure is a more difficult exploration, and it concerns an elusive and lonely vocation. In a structure which is at best neutral and frequently antipathetic to the popularly held notions of Christianity, the layman often finds that he must exercise his ministry without conscious support from the Church, and without revealing his motivation. As three laymen said to the New Delhi meeting of the World Council of Churches:

We sometimes have the feeling that you have little understanding for our solidarity with our non-Christian neighbors and colleagues. . . . You often press us to become quite consciously the light of the world, to be known as Christians, to form Christian cells in the world of our work and neighborhoods. Often such reminders are quite necessary. But more often our Christian obedience demands us to remain *incognito* and thus to serve Christ. It may then happen that suddenly, to the amazement of our non-Christian friends, the light of Christ reflects itself in us. It is then not our work but his, not our light but his.[11]

The concern for relevant ministry is a sign of great promise within the Church. Surely God will use it for his own ends, in his own way. There is a serious danger, however, particularly in the United States, that the sheer institutionalism of American Christianity will domesticate the concern for lay ministry, overlaying it with the pious religiosity which is a vestige of our attachment to a defunct Christendom. Ministry in the new age *must* take place within the structures of the age; when and in what fashion are the as yet unanswered questions.[12]

3. *Church order in the abundant society.* The parish church as we know it is a creature of another age and culture. What shape the worshiping community will take in the future is an idle speculation. The important fact is that some adaptation is inevitable. In the newer countries of Africa and Asia it is already apparent that the Western parish structure cannot function. An ordained ministry supported by the gifts of a congregation is beyond the means of local communities in many places, even if sufficient clergy are available. In the United States, the multiplication of expensive church facilities, particularly on a competitive denominational basis, outstrips the financial resources of dioceses or church boards. Rapid population growth will increase the difficulties of church extension along the lines of the past.

Engagement of the principalities and powers of the age demands an even more searching analysis of the Church's corporate life. Traditional lines of denominational separation make little or no sense at the point of contact with human ethical issues in society. Tactically, we are already learning the value of ecumenical co-operation on social issues. The thaw within Roman Catholicism holds out the promise of a joint Christian witness unknown since the medieval period. The likelihood that worshiping communities will develop within the world of work as in the residential neighborhood; the growth of "guild" relationships, whether formally or spontaneously; the necessity for at least some of the ordained clergy to earn their primary income in "secular" jobs; the withering away of many of the activities of the typical parish church; the actual decline in attendance and church membership in the United States following the comparable experience of Europe and Great Britain —all these are prospects of the next generation. They augur an era in which the nominal adherence to Christianity will be in decline. In the judgment of Almighty God, they may well hold the promise of a recovery of relevant ministry, theological growth, and significant engagement with the abundant world which God has opened to the children of men.

# ➤ PART II

# Threats to the Society of Abundance

## 5

# THE THREATS OF STAGNATION AND STARVATION

### by David Horowitz

Two-thirds of humanity today live at or below subsistence level.
This is the most crucial problem of our time. It transcends in
importance and gravity all other social and economic problems
of the century. It is the living symbol of the fact that the disparities in the economy of the world are clearly the most disrup-
tive agents working against the achievement of world order and
peace through a world community.

The rift between the two giant power blocs is mainly an
ideological one resulting from the different ways in which they
view their economies and from the different social patterns that
these different economies have created. These economic disparities are a breeding ground for growing world antagonism.

In many of the developed countries, class conflicts on a
national scale dwindle into insignificance thanks to the welfare
state, built-in stabilizers, fiscal and monetary policies, and so
forth. The economic conflicts are now not national but regional.
The economic gaps between the developed and the underdeveloped nations are incomparably greater than any that exist between the social classes within the developed countries.

77

Ideological concepts persist long after the economic basis for their existence disappears. Semantics and intellectual orthodoxy perpetuate them. This is true both of class conflicts in the highly developed welfare states and of the anticolonial reactions in the underdeveloped countries to colonialism in its crude form of political domination and economic exploitation.

The disparities that lie at the root of the economic problems of our time are paradoxical. In the highly developed countries, lack of demand slows down production and full capacity is frequently not utilized; in the underdeveloped countries, production lags behind demand.

The terms of trade favor manufactured products the prices of which rise or at least are maintained, as prices of primary commodities fall behind. Productivity in agriculture is lagging where its increase is most imperative and is relatively lowest where the proportion of agricultural population is greatest. Increase in agricultural production is highest where stocks of food are already excessive. Growth of population and the demographic explosion are most pronounced where malnutrition prevails. Shortage of capital is worst where capital is most needed. The rate of saving is lowest where new investments are most imperative, for the simple reason that saving is lowest where incomes are at or below subsistence level.

The pronounced difference in liquidity between nations as well as short-term capital movements create disparities in the balance of payments among various national economic units, impairing the exchange of goods and services.

The disparities are clearly reflected in the fact that the share of the United States, Western Europe, and Japan in the total national incomes of seventy of the states affiliated with the International Monetary Fund (which represent a large cross section of the world) is 75 per cent, although these three areas represent only 25 per cent of the population of all of the countries within the Fund.

Demography, terms of trade, difficulty of capital formation in less developed countries, and paucity of capital imports—all combine to aggravate the human, political, and economic implications of the problem.

Despite the technological progress of modern times, there may be more poverty-stricken people in the world today than there were fifty or a hundred years ago.

## CHAINING THE MALTHUSIAN DEVIL

The disparity in economic standards and in stages of economic development is aggravated by demography. The specter evoked by Malthus is rising again. Frequently, development is unable to catch up with the rapid increase of population. Standards of life in countries where the population pressure on limited resources is greatest cannot be further depressed without grave consequences. We are living in "the period of demographic explosion." At the present rate of increase, the world population will double every forty-two years, and will total some six billion by the end of the century.

The pressure of growing populations on scarce resources is accentuated in countries that are already densely populated. In 1949, the national income in Europe generally ranged between $350 and $800 per capita, but in Asia it was $50 to $100 per capita.

A paradox appears in this demographic discrepancy: the more extensive and more developed are health services and hygienic progress, the graver the population problem. The main factor in the rapid increase of the population is not a rise in the birth rate but a decline in the mortality rate, which in some underdeveloped countries has dropped 30 to 60 per cent in one decade. In some countries with the highest rate of reproduction in human history, the population doubles every twenty-two to twenty-five years. Preventive medicine, more hygienic methods, and the increasing use of vaccination, sulfa drugs, and antibiotics, and D.D.T. as a remedy against the spread of malaria are radically reducing the mortality rates, particularly among infants. And while the death rate falls rapidly, the birth rate remains high.

This extraordinary increase in population takes place in the underdeveloped nations in spite of the appalling poverty and low standards of life reflected in a life expectancy at birth of 32.5 years for males and 31.7 years for females in India (1941-50), in comparison with some 67 to 70 years in the highly developed countries of Europe and America. In countries in which the decline in the death rate is gradual, it is usually accompanied by simultaneous changes in mental, psychological, and cultural attitudes leading to a declining birth rate. It is obvious, however, that if the process is very rapid and revolutionary, the changes cannot keep pace with the new developments and the decline of the birth rate thus lags behind the decline of the death rate. Production cannot keep up with the rapid increase of population, and so living standards of life do not rise in these countries. Moreover, changes in the birth rate through conscious control of procreation are subject to cultural and psychological as well as social and religious influences, which are generally rigid and conservative.

The vicious circle of uncontrolled demographic expansion and declining standards of life is thus closing. The imbalance of population on a world scale is being accentuated by growing differences in per capita incomes.

Eugene Black, president of the World Bank, warned recently that all the efforts of industrial countries could be nullified if population in the poorer countries continues to grow at its present rate of 2 to 3.5 per cent a year. He maintains that to point to the favorable economic effects of a growing population is "widely irrelevant" to the problems of most developing countries today. "We are coming to a situation in which the optimist will be the man who thinks that present living standards can be maintained."

These circumstances explain the efforts of the underdeveloped nations to chain the Malthusian devil as a precondition to the rise of living standards. Otherwise, an increase of the gross national product may be vitiated by an excessive increase of population.

## PRICE PATTERN

Another disparity is the result of the price pattern and price fluctuations in a modern economy. The changes in prices of primary commodities as a group have been about 50 to 55 per cent greater than those of manufactures as a group. While the prices of manufactured products have been maintained or even risen, the prices of primary products have continuously declined. This fact has created balance-of-payment difficulties for the primary-producing countries, particularly in view of their fixed obligations. The decline reflects long-term structural trends and is not a problem that arises only in connection with general cyclical fluctuations in the world economy. We are faced with some basic structural changes.

Since 1951, the underlying world trend of prices of primary commodities, measured in the aggregate, has been irregularly but steeply downward. And since 1957 there has been a decline of nearly 5 per cent in the prices of exports of the countries producing primary commodities. The net loss after deducting the decline of prices of imported products in these countries in the year 1958 alone exceeded the total financial assistance received in that year by the less developed countries.

Even in times of boom in the highly developed industrial countries, there was no improvement in the terms of trade for the underdeveloped nations. The decline in prices has a cumulative effect because price declines discourage large stock holdings, and the unloading of these stocks further enforces the downward trend of prices. Thus, while the trend of the 1930s was reversed in almost every other respect in the postwar period, surpluses of primary commodities have continued to depress their price levels.

The underdeveloped nations of the world are caught in the scissors of declining prices of primary produce and rising costs of manufactured commodities and of capital equipment required for their development.

## DEVELOPMENT AND DEMOCRACY

The first industrial revolution was based on a very high rate of savings and private accumulation of capital. The distribution of the national income in those times was instrumental in accelerating the formation of capital, by assuring a high rate of profit and by keeping wage rates on levels just sufficient for the maintenance and reproduction of the labor force. These wage levels were possible because there was always a reserve army of unemployed workers to be called on. It was a dismal, grim period and amply illustrated the theory of the iron wage law. The conditions were possible only within the framework of a society in which democracy was in a nascent state and the broad masses of the population were either deprived of political influence or inarticulate.

This performance was repeated in the U.S.S.R. after the 1917 revolution. The very existence of the new regime depended on rapid economic progress. Speedy industrialization, occupational reshuffles, and large-scale urbanization were possible only by a fast formation of capital through forced savings, and the totalitarian regime was strong, stern, and severe enough to enforce this solution. Today Red China is trying to achieve similar results by lowering consumption and enforcing saving.

There is one common feature between the early capitalism of the industrial revolution in England and Western Europe, on one hand, and the Soviet regime and the economic system of Red China in the postwar period, on the other. This is a very rapid capital formation through cruel and ruthless restraint of consumption and reduction in living standards. Such an economic policy can be enforced only in a predemocratic or totalitarian regime. Its concomitants are the appalling poverty and starvation of early capitalism and the extremely low standards of life in totalitarian regimes in the initial period of their development.

The process of primary formation of capital under these circumstances is extremely slow in underdeveloped countries and is made even more difficult by the increasing pressure of population growth. The propensity to save is, of course, reduced if the population expands more rapidly than the national income, so that real income per capita decreases. The rate of saving will be low because of the relatively small excess of real income over and above the subsistence level. The process of accumulation is further retarded by the fact that institutional saving in these countries is in its embryonic stage and the use of money as a medium of exchange is limited.

The margin above bare existence in these populations is so small as to defy any attempt to squeeze out of them savings for capital formation and subsequent investment. They cannot lift themselves by the straps of their own boots. In addition, political and social factors will militate against a policy of forced savings so long as consumption levels are distressingly low.

Theoretically such a policy could be put into effect by heavy taxation, extremely low wages, and the introduction of what would practically amount to forced labor in village communities, but the resistance to these measures in any but totalitarian regimes would be so formidable as to defeat their ends. They would be even more difficult to apply nowadays because of the "demonstration effect" of Western civilization and living standards. The modern media of mass communication, even the shining car crossing an appallingly poor village in India or Egypt, conjure up the picture of a better life that is not solely confined to keeping body and soul together. This is the new revolution of rising expectations.

Thus, an attempt to execute a policy of rapid capital formation in these countries could only be achieved by coercion, and a totalitarian regime would be much more efficient and effective in it. Under a democratic system, moreover, in an economy run on the basis of a multiplicity of private decisions of employers, factory owners, landlords, and the like, there would be no certainty, and perhaps little probability, that the resources that would be created by depressing living standards and decreasing consumption would be diverted to investment.

The sheer accumulation of capital does not guarantee that it will be used for investment and the promotion of economic growth. In some of the underdeveloped countries a small but wealthy minority at the top of the ladder has considerable resources in its hands and squanders most of them in conspicuous consumption. This is particularly the case in the Middle East, with its immense income from oil royalties. England of the industrial revolution used its accumulated resources for investment in order to expand its production capacity, but this does not mean that the same course of action will be followed in Saudi Arabia. The will to apply resources properly, knowledge, skill, and entrepreneurial initiative are the indispensable prerequisites of economic growth.

## TRANSFER OF CAPITAL

Import of capital and forced accumulation of savings are interchangeable. Help from outside sources is the only possible substitute for forced formation of capital. The alternative to both is economic stagnation. The problem of large-scale capital transfer must be viewed, first and foremost, from the angle of the capital market in countries able to export capital. The worldwide shortage of capital is becoming one of the most decisive and influential factors in the economic pattern of the world. The pressure of demand for capital is accentuated by powerful new economic, technical, political, and sociological developments in this postwar "age of dislocation and experiment."

First, the second industrial revolution. Automation, or the replacement of labor by machines; the electronic industry, spreading out new, hitherto unknown branches, as an auxiliary arm of armament and a source of new needs through communications; the use of atomic energy for industrial purposes— all of these need immense capital investment. They deeply affect general economic conditions because of the competitive advantage possessed by enterprises with a high component of fixed capital and the consequent need of other enterprises to accelerate their pace of re-equipment in order to reach the same objective. Thus, the new industrial revolution works in two directions: quicker obsolescence and a need for re-equipment of whole industries, and a higher unit of fixed capital per unit of production. Re-equipment is being accelerated. The volume of capital to be used for this purpose in the United States alone in 1960 was estimated at $38 billion.

Second, rearmament. The immense needs of rearmament coincide with the new industrial revolution and create an additional claim on existing resources. Moreover, the developments in this field parallel those of industry in general—less manpower, more fixed assets (long-range aircraft, ballistic missiles, etc.), and vast quantities of capital equipment.

Third, the rising curve of world population. The world's 2.7 billion population has almost doubled in the past seventy years and is expected to redouble in the next forty-two years. This stupendous growth generates new needs in housing, schools, roads, and, last but not least, capital equipment for the integration of the population into the machinery of production.

From the supply side, the flow of capital to investment is being diminished by the redistribution of national income, which reduces higher-bracket incomes, a large part of which were accumulated and invested, and raises middle and low incomes. This results not only in the elimination of social extremes but also in an increase in aggregate consumption because of the rising living standards of those sections of the population which have a higher propensity to consume. Under conditions of full employment this rise in living standards decreases the share of income saved, accumulated, and invested and increases the share of income consumed.

Thus, the rate of accumulation is decreasing through social progress as a smaller share of income is saved and accumulated. This social transformation has invalidated the nineteenth-century prognosis of social polarization. Today the economic and social gap between the worker and the employer in developed countries is much less pronounced than that between the worker in developed countries and the worker in underdeveloped areas.

The supply of capital is also reduced by the bargaining power of trade unions, which affects the internal supply of capital in highly developed countries and has an even more powerful impact on the export of capital to underdeveloped countries. This leads to a conflict of social and economic interests between the trade-union movement in the developed nations and the vast populations of underdeveloped areas. It results in a diminished rate of savings and capital accumulation; higher consumption with a larger internal market and greater and more varied and attractive possibilities of investment in developed countries; accentuation of discrepancies between the prices of primary commodities produced by underdeveloped countries and the prices of manufactured products in the highly industrialized nations; and a rise in the price of capital equipment needed for the development of underdeveloped nations.

Of course, this clash of interests is not conscious and deliberate. The workers in the developed lands are among the ardent supporters of aid to underdeveloped countries. The rather indirect influence on the possibilities of export of capital of rising living standards and increased consumption caused by rising wage levels is too complicated a phenomenon to be understood by many people concerned with their own individual problems. So far as the great mass of people are concerned, the esoteric character of intricate economic processes and the many ramifications and indirect impacts of various socio-economic measures are unknown or ignored. It is impossible to gauge what the attitude of the labor movement would be if the contradiction between ideology and vested interests were raised to the level of political consciousness and action.

The expectation of an easy capital market after a period of reconstruction following World War II has not materialized. A chain of technological discoveries and a booming home market in the mature economies of the West claim a growing share of capital for their own investment needs, leaving only small surpluses for export to underdeveloped countries. The annual report of the World Bank mentions the "heavy investment demand which pressed with increasing force on the available supply of savings." The claim of developed countries on existing resources for new investment is expected to increase.

The theoretical assumption that the surplus of capital in the Western economies is attracted because of higher potential returns to countries with underdeveloped resources, cheap labor, and unexploited sources of raw materials has not come true. Insecurity of the capital invested is only one of the factors against extensive exports of capital to underdeveloped countries. The low productivity of the labor force as well as its lack of skills likewise discourages foreign investment. An expanding and diversified market, coupled with increasing demand, exerts a pull on capital to invest in already industrialized countries. The existence of auxiliary industries, of scientific institutions, and of all kinds of technical facilities is an additional stimulant to such investment. Capital is reluctant to break virgin ground in unexplored and undeveloped areas when the lure of profitable investment in developed countries is so great.

Another attraction of the developed and industrialized countries is their money and capital market, with ample credit facilities, on the one hand and, on the other, the high liquidity of investment in shares wherever the stock exchange serves as an efficient instrument for shifting from liquid to fixed and from fixed to liquid assets. Except for the capital going to underdeveloped countries to exploit their oil resources, little is flowing according to the natural processes of economic gravitation, and even this amount is affected to some extent by artificial stimuli, such as the activity of the World Bank, grants-in-aid, and so on.

## LIMITED USE OF RESOURCES

Still another disparity making for international economic disequilibrium appears in the underutilization of productive capacity in highly developed nations at the same time that the demand for capital equipment in the underdeveloped countries remains unsatisfied.

Full use of existing resources in highly developed countries could be greatly facilitated by export of capital. Increasing productivity and far-reaching mechanization and automation are already causing technological unemployment in the United

States. Even in parts of Europe, increase in employment lags behind all other economic indicators. The diversion of resources in the developed countries to the production of commodities to satisfy artificially created needs has recently provoked much adverse comment because it is happening where conditions in the underdeveloped nations are desperate and their ameliora-tion should be our paramount interest.

The "bogey of maturity" arises in the highly developed sec-tions of the world with the gradual widening of the margin be-tween production capacity and actual output. Stimulating the export of capital to underdeveloped nations or increasing in-ternal expenditures, mainly through governmental channels, are the alternative solutions to this problem.

Prolonged recessions involving a high rate of unemployment are now being prevented by deliberate stimulation of the do-mestic market. But even in their present mild form, mitigated by built-in stabilizers, the cost of recessions in terms of under-employed resources is high. The Council of Economic Advisers found that "the gap between actual and potential output for 1960 as a whole can . . . be estimated at 30-35 billion dollars, or 6 to 7 per cent of total output. . . . Even the most pros-perous nation cannot afford to waste resources on this scale."

Banning the "bogey of maturity" and reducing the margin of underemployed resources could be important by-products of large-scale investment in underdeveloped nations.

One suggestion for such investment is to allocate a certain proportion of the Gross National Product of the industrialized countries to that purpose. One and a half per cent of the GNP of the developed nations is about $15 billion. The interest of developed nations in such a plan is reinforced by the structural changes in mature economies.

The most pronounced swings and cyclical fluctuations occur in the production of capital equipment and durable goods. They are the most vulnerable sectors of modern economies and frequently are the sources of recession or economic slack. Heavy industries producing capital equipment and durable goods obviously occupy a key position in cyclical developments. A balanced growth, therefore, depends upon a rising curve of production in heavy industry producing capital equipment. In periods of economic recession in the United States after World War II, the decline was most pronounced in the durable-goods sector. This seems to be the key to the prevention of cyclical crises and recessions.

However, we are confronted with certain realities. The flow of capital to those areas which are most in need of it is still very limited, as we have said. These are mostly countries with growing populations pressing on limited resources. They are clearly not the most attractive areas for investment of capital and can hardly be expected to compete with more developed economies on the capital market of the world.

## HOT MONEY

All the disparities that we have described so far are accentuated by disparities in the balance of payments and differences in liquidity among the various countries. They result from the fact that although the supply of money in each country is determined by the fiscal policies of the government of that country and the monetary policies of central banks, no such control exists in the international arena where the flow of capital is erratic and independent of conscious direction. Within a short period of time the world experienced the dollar gap,

then the sterling crisis and the dollar crisis, and later the
sterling crisis again. The abolition of the gold standard com-
pelled each country to organize its own control of the money
supply. But as long as there is no such organization interna-
tionally, financial disparities are inevitable.

Short-term capital movements, mostly speculative, that clog
the channels of trade and certain internal policies of national
units lead to fluctuations and lack of equilibrium in international financial and trade relations. The new method of
managed currency encounters the pitfalls of the sorcerer's ap-
prentice. The uninitiated playing with forces and formulae
they do not fully understand can easily and even inadvertently
open the Pandora box of inflation. The problem is one of balance between effective demand created by the supply of money
and actual or potential supply of goods and services.

Government-induced monetary expansion is frequently the
result of a genuine desire to accelerate the process of badly
needed economic development. In a country with dormant
factors of production or underutilized resources, this policy may
even be successful in the short run by galvanizing idle capacity.
Eventually, however, the acquisition of resources by the state
through inflation defeats its own purpose. As the surplus purchasing power spills over into excessive demand for foreign
currency with which to buy imported goods because even increased domestic production cannot satisfy the new demand,
rising price levels and greater pressure on the balance of payments must lead to a deterioration of the economy. Depletion
of the reserves of foreign currency, physical shortages, and unemployment caused by lack of raw materials and other com-
ponents of production dependent on imports are the inevitable
results.

## IN CONCLUSION

The central problem, on which the future of humanity may depend, is to eliminate economic disparities throughout the world. This has become possible in our time because the blind incalculable economic forces are being increasingly superseded by conscious economic policies and controls. Wiser monetary and fiscal policies, the growth and impact of the welfare state, built-in stabilizers—all contribute to the new pattern of a balanced economy. Modern technology is a great contributing factor in making such control possible.

The three chief predictions of the nineteenth century by both classical and Marxist economists—increasing impoverishment, unavoidable cyclical crises, and the compelling need for economic imperialism—have been disproved by the realities of our time.

The questions we face are these:

1. How can economic controls be made effective within a framework of free democratic decisions?

2. How can formation of capital be supplemented by transfer of capital?

3. How can short-term movements of capital and difficulties in balance of payments be neutralized by institutional, worldwide arrangements?

4. How can fluctuations of boom and recession be smoothed out on a national and international scale?

5. How can the population explosion be mitigated by family planning?

The tools for answering these questions and for developing a worldwide economic policy are available. The economic forces that caused the 1929 crisis can now be controlled. There is no need for a perilous and pernicious pessimism. A projection of the welfare state onto the international scene and transformation of the community of nations into a world welfare community would eliminate the gravest of disparities.

The struggle for world peace is a race against time. Today the rift between the power blocs rooted in differences between their economic ideologies seems to be unbridgeable, but the actual gap between the economic regimes is decreasing all the time. The growing reliance on market forces in the Soviet bloc and the growing consciousness of the need for direction and planning in the Western world are leading to some degree of assimilation of the different economic systems. Some day it may seem absurd to fight wars or to hurl nuclear weapons around because there happen to be technical differences in the methods of economic control between one group of countries and another.

For men who are now reaching for the stars it should not be beyond their power to eliminate economic disparities. Their ability to accomplish this end depends only on one simple thing: their will to do so.

## 6 ☙

# THE THREAT OF ANNIHILATION

### ☙ by Surendra J. Patel

Throughout the history of humanity, chiefs, kings, emperors, and nation states have all relied on warfare to protect and, if possible, to expand their domination. Major advances in techniques have often found their first application in means of conquest—no less true today than at the height of the power of ancient Egypt, Sumer, China, India, and Peru. The continuing reliance on weapons of warfare has now as never before reached the point of logical absurdity. Armaments in the arsenals of the major powers are capable of annihilating most of mankind. Realization that war between them could no longer serve as an instrument of national policy is spreading. And yet, arms are being piled up. Like the miserly person hiding under the floor the savings he would neither use nor bequeath, nations are adding to an ever expanding stockpile of weapons even a small part of which is adequate to destroy all, including themselves.

There is now an accumulation of technical knowledge which in an outburst of half an hour of insanity could devastate almost all animate objects, the product of patient evolution over the ages. But if wisely utilized, it also has the potential to overcome in half a century the age-old afflictions of mankind— squalor, poverty, want, and disease. Humanity is thus being steadily pressed to choose between half an hour of insanity or half a century of farsighted international co-operation.

These mounting pressures were reflected in resolution 1378 (XIV) of the General Assembly of the United Nations in 1959. In it, the question of disarmament was characterized as "the most important one facing the world today." It expressed the hope that "measures leading towards the goal of general and complete disarmament under effective international control will be worked out in detail and agreed upon in the shortest possible time." This urgency for disarmament symbolized the universal desire to assure human survival.

A disarmed world would presuppose political accommodation among nations. Continued heavy military expenditures have become almost an economic habit, acting like a tranquilizer for national nervousness born of insecurity. To redeploy the resources now devoted to armaments would create important problems of adjustments for individuals, countries, and the entire world economy. An advance study of these problems could therefore be of considerable help in overcoming the difficulties of, and in deriving the maximum benefits from, disarmament.

In pursuance of the General Assembly resolution 1516 (XV), a group of experts was appointed by the United Nations to study the problems of transition to a disarmed world. In its report, *The Economic and Social Consequences of Disarmament*, the group was "unanimously of the opinion that all the problems and difficulties of transition connected with disarmament could be met by appropriate national and international measures."

This article draws heavily upon the findings of the consultative group. Their unanimity of views was underlined by Acting Secretary-General U Thant, in his preface to the report. He stated: "It is a source of profound gratification to me, as I am sure it will be to all governments, that, on a subject that has until recently been so beset by ideological differences it has now proved possible for a group of experts drawn from countries with different economic systems and at different stages of economic development to reach unanimous agreement."

The members of the group were: V. Y. Aboltin, Deputy Director, Institute of World Economics and International Relations, Academy of Sciences of the U.S.S.R.; Mamoun Beheiry, Governor, Bank of Sudan; Arthur J. Brown, Head, Department of Economics, University of Leeds, England; B. N. Ganguli, Head, the Delhi School of Economics, India; Aftab Ahmad Khan, Chief Economist, Planning Commission, Pakistan; Oskar Lange, Chairman, Economic Council, Council of Ministers of the People's Republic of Poland; W. W. Leontief, Professor of Economics, Harvard University, United States; Jose Antonio Mayobre, Ambassador of Venezuela to the United States; and Alfred Sauvy, Director, National Institute of Demographic Studies, Government of France. Mr. Sauvy was represented at the meetings of the second session of the group by Paul Paillat, also of the National Institute of Demographic Studies.

## MAIN FEATURES OF MILITARY
## EXPENDITURES

*The burden of armaments.* A study of the economics of disarmament requires an assessment of the resources which are at present devoted to military expenditures. Owing to a number of limitations of data, such as the difference in the coverage of defense budgets, in comparative prices for equipment, in the scale of pay for armed forces, etc., it is not easy to assess them adequately. On the basis of the available data, the United Nations consultative group suggested that the world appears to be spending roughly $120 billion annually on military expenditure. This is equal to about 8 to 9 per cent of the world's annual output, or to at least two-thirds of the entire national income of the underdeveloped countries. It is close to the value of the world exports of all commodities, and slightly lower than the total resources that are devoted to net capital formation in the whole world. Nearly twenty million men now serve in the world's armed forces. When other persons occupied directly or indirectly in servicing the needs of these armies are added to them, the total may well run over fifty million.

The volume of resources devoted to military expenditure during the last decade of relative peace is indeed impressive. The world has spent more on the instruments of international intimidation in this short period than on education since the beginning of the age of enlightenment three centuries ago. Total military expenditures in the last ten years amounted to nearly $1,200 billion. This sum is about seven times the annual income and seventy times the annual net investment of the underdeveloped countries. As a rough and ready estimate, it may be suggested that if it had been devoted to the economic development of these countries, it could have raised the volume of their reproducible assets in industries and in the modernized sectors twelvefold, and their total capital assets nearly threefold. Their annual per-capita income could have been raised three times. Poverty could thus have become a pastime for the historians, and later for the archeologists.

*Concentration of defense outlays.* The heavy military burden is not spread evenly all over the world. It is concentrated in only a handful of countries, and within each of them in a limited number of sectors of employment and geographical locations.

The United Nations group of experts estimated that only seven countries—Canada, West Germany, France, China, the U.S.S.R., the United Kingdom, and the United States—account for nearly 85 per cent of this. At the other end of the spectrum, the underdeveloped countries are responsible for nearly 5 per cent of the world total. All of them together spend for this purpose nearly as much as the United Kingdom alone. Military expenditures are, in fact, much more heavily concentrated in a few countries than world income or investments.

Among the major military powers, production as well as employment depending on military ends is also highly concentrated in a few industrial sectors—for example, munitions, electrical machinery, instruments and related products, and transport equipment (including airplanes and missiles). More often than not such dependence is centered in a particular locality or region within a given country.

This heavy concentration of military expenditures in a limited number of countries, industries, and localities would have considerable significance in outlining the economic effects of disarmament. Once they are identified, this could facilitate the formulation of concrete measures that might be necessary to counteract the probable depressing economic impact of reduced military expenditures.

Most of the underdeveloped countries devote less than 4 per cent of their resources to military expenditures. A large part of these consists of payment of salaries and provision of food and clothing for the armies. The resources that these countries devote to military hardware are relatively small, and a significant portion of financing often comes from abroad. Disarmament would therefore have a relatively limited direct impact on the flow of physical output in these countries. (The influence of world disarmament on their exports is, however, a very important consideration, which is discussed later.) Insofar as some countries have to spend their own precious foreign-exchange resources to import military equipment, disarmament would enable them to transfer these to imports of much needed capital equipment.

## THE EXPERIENCE OF POSTWAR DISARMAMENT

The elimination of armaments from national arsenals would obviously depend on political understanding among the major powers. But the man in the street is often concerned about whether countries can really afford to disarm. This genuine concern symbolizes the individual fear of losing a job without finding another. It focuses attention at a national level on the apprehensions about maintaining full employment in countries which may have become used to armaments as an economic drug. There is also uncertainty about whether the economic and political leadership which so readily allocates resources for military purposes would be equally willing, ready, and prompt to divert them toward much more beneficial social and other ends.

An advance analysis of the problems involved in the process of transition to disarmed economies is therefore of considerable importance. Drawing on the experience of such a transition at the end of World War II can set the stage for the discussion of the problems which countries with different economic systems and at different stages of economic growth would now face in the event of disarmament.

During the closing years of the last war, many countries devoted nearly half their resources to mutual destruction. The number of men in uniform and the real volume of military expenditure were four times as high as today. The destructive preoccupations of these years left in their trail the terrible signs of sick humanity—millions dead and mutilated; homes, hospitals, and factories destroyed; productive assets paralyzed; communications dislocated; the network of trade disrupted; currencies without confidence; and people in despair. And yet, huge armies were quickly demobilized with almost no rise in the level of unemployment. Plants producing armaments were rapidly turned to the output of articles of everyday use. The visible scars of war were soon healed.

The experience of conversion may be illustrated by some examples. In 1946, the military expenditure in the United States was reduced to just about one-fifth of the level of only one year before. Between August 1945 and June 1946, over nine million men gave up the army uniform for civilian clothes. In the United Kingdom, seven million persons engaged either in the army or in servicing it were released in a matter of sixteen months. But in both the countries a very rapid expansion of output for civilian purposes opened up sufficient employment opportunities so that unemployment, contrary to the predictions of many economists, increased but little. In continental Western Europe, war destruction and dislocation were much greater. Most commodities were in short supply. Inflationary pressures were severe. Confidence in currencies was shaken. But in eighteen months after the end of the hostilities, industrial output rose to the prewar level nearly everywhere, except in Western Germany and Italy.

The Soviet Union and the eastern European countries had suffered most severe human and material losses. Vast numbers of peoples were moved far away from their normal places of residence. Despite these incredible handicaps the prewar level of industrial output was reached or surpassed by 1948.

The destruction, devastation, and dislocation caused by the war were very severe. The total resources devoted to the war were far greater than at present. But the destructiveness of the war was more than matched by the resilience of the economies. This process of very rapid conversion has provided the countries with a valuable experience. Referring to the measures adopted during the process of conversion, the United States government stated that "tried measures such as these would be under active consideration again in the event of the acceptance of a disarmament program."

The ease as well as the rapid pace of the conversion at the end of the war was no doubt due to special circumstances. A decade and a half of the Great Depression and the war had created a vast backlog of demand for both consumption and investment. Liquid savings in the hands of the population and enterprises were devoted to buying things as soon as they became available. The major concern of economic policy was to curb, rather than to maintain—let alone to stimulate—effective demand.

This particular difference between the early postwar and the present setting was sharply underlined by the recession which was associated with the reduction of about $10 billion in military spending in the United States between 1953 and 1954. Governments are now aware that the special factors of postwar conversion are no longer present. The government of the United States, for instance, stated:

Despite the mildness of the 1954 recession, it now is clear that fiscal and monetary policies might have been applied with more vigor. The reason they were not is that the decline in defense spending following the Korean war was not treated by the policymakers as a major demobilization requiring strong compensatory action. For this reason the 1953-54 period does not provide a significant guide to the behavior of the American economy in a disarmament program during the 1960s.

It may be expected therefore that this awareness would prove conducive toward adopting effective measures during future disarmament.


TURNING SWORDS INTO PLOWSHARES

Mankind's first step toward a disarmed world would not be like sailing in already charted waters. He would encounter a number of new problems while turning the swords into plowshares. Attention may be drawn to three of them which merit advance study: the maintenance of the over-all level of economic activity or, in more familiar words, avoiding a recession or a depression which would increase unemployment; minimizing and counteracting the adverse economic effects in particular industries, localities, or regions caused by the elimination of certain activities serving military uses; and overcoming the disturbance that a decline in the military demand for certain imported materials may cause to the economies which depend on exporting them for their foreign-exchange earnings.

In many respects economic growth of nations also involves solving problems which are not altogether different. Major advances in technology and changes in the level and the pattern of output and demand necessitate continual reallocation of resources of labor and productive equipment among occupations, industries, and regions. Output of some industries expands while that of others contracts. Some regions, once prosperous, lose in importance and become economically depressed. The faster the growth of an economy, the easier it has been to carry out many of these adjustments. The economic impact of disarmament, while embracing similar phenomena, would be somewhat different because of two important considerations. Unlike unplanned economic growth, many of the problems that would be encountered in the process of conversion are now being studied in advance. International organizations, governments, and individual research establishments are already outlining plans and programs to cope with the dislocations that may arise. Second, and in a more important sense, disarmament would release vast resources, now employed toward destructive ends, to help surmount the problems it would create. Thus, disarmament in fact would facilitate overcoming its own dislocations.

*Avoiding a recession.* How would the reduction in military expenditure be carried out? The answer to this question would, to a large extent, determine whether it would lead to a recession or give additional stimulus to economic growth. If reduction in military expenditures leads to a fall in over-all purchasing power, there is little doubt that it will reduce the level of economic activity and increase unemployment. But it would hardly be a tribute to the caliber of economic management if falling demand were to culminate in a recession. On the other hand, if a reduction in military expenditure were balanced by an equivalent expansion of other forms of demand, there need be no short fall in over-all demand. The offsetting expansion could take the form of increases in personal consumption, private investment, and public expenditure for domestic ends as well as for foreign aid to the developing countries. The task of economic policy would be to ensure an expansion in other sectors which would offset the decline in military expenditures.

Since the Great Depression, considerable advances have been made in solving the problems of maintaining effective demand in the private-enterprise economies. The United Nations group of experts, drawing attention to this aspect, stated in their report:

> Member countries are pledged under the United Nations Charter to maintain full employment. A number of Governments have further undertaken, in national statements of policy, to adopt measures toward that objective. The instruments available for the prevention of any substantial fall of demand are well known. Their relative merits, however, vary widely from one country to another and from one time to another because of differences in institutions and attitudes.

The various instruments of policy that could be used to sustain the level of economic activity include the reduction of income taxes, indirect taxes on mass consumption goods, measures to stimulate investment, reduction of public debt, and expansion of government expenditure. Following an analysis of the relative merits of these, the experts concluded that "disarmament need not therefore increase the difficulty of economic stabilization in the industrialized private enterprise economies."

In the centrally planned economies, the major economic decisions concerning consumption, investment, and public expenditures are co-ordinated through a central plan. The maintenance of the level of economic activity during the processes of conversion in these countries would therefore "be simply a matter of economic efficiency of planning techniques," according to the report. For one form of expenditure, such as military outlays, could be substituted other forms, such as investment, consumption, and foreign assistance. The precise manner of allocating resources among these forms would be determined by "the physical adaptation of plants producing armaments to the production of goods for civilian use," suggests the report.

*Structural problems of conversion.* Even when the countries succeed in maintaining the over-all level of economic activity during the conversion, they would be faced with important problems of adjustments in specific industrial sectors and geographical areas. In some cases, the adaptation might be relatively easy: for instance, a shift from the production of tanks to tractors, of military to civilian aircraft, of naval vessels to merchant ships. The changes in the plant and equipment, and in the number and in the skills of the employees would be small in these cases. On the other hand, there would be instances where disarmament would necessitate major adjustments in the pattern of output and employment in specific economic fields or regions. Many sectors of employment, for instance the ordnance factories or the armed forces, might be eliminated completely. The people employed in these would have to seek work in other sectors, often located at different centers. This would thus involve the movement of people to different locations.

Hypothetical estimates about the changes in employment called forth by complete disarmament, under various assumptions concerning reallocation of resources, have been prepared for two countries—the United States and the United Kingdom. These calculations suggest that if the processes of disarmament were spread over a number of years "the change per annum would be only a fraction of the total." In countries with labor shortages, disarmament would release manpower for accelerating economic growth.

The group of experts also analyzed a number of special problems arising from the concentration of military effort in certain sectors and areas. These related to adaptation of skills to peacetime requirements: problems of assistance to particular enterprises, industries, and localities heavily oriented to military use; and reorientation of research and technological development. In general they were of the opinion that the resources released by disarmament would be so large that, given advanced planning and vigorous policy, it should be possible to overcome these dislocations.

*Influence on foreign trade.* Disarmament would reflect a lessening of international tensions, a rebuilding of confidence between the private-enterprise economies and the centrally planned economies, and would improve the economic relations between them. This would contribute to the expansion of trade between them, and higher economic activity in the wake of disarmament would help to expand international trade in general.

An acceleration of economic growth would also stimulate the

demand for primary products. But in some countries the fall
in military demand for particular commodities might cause
difficulties. Military expenditures account for a significant part
of demand for many primary products, such as copper, tin,
nickel, lead, zinc, and petroleum, and their prices are very
sensitive to changes in demand. The combined unfavorable
influences of a decline in the volume of demand as well as
in prices could affect adversely those countries whose exports
consist largely of these items.

Since the fall in military demand would be offset by a rise
in civilian and other forms of public demand, the experts felt
that disarmament would have only a small effect on the over-all
demand for these commodities. Should particular difficulties
be faced by some countries, however, they emphasized the need
for special aid to them:

> For many of the countries mainly dependent on the export of
> primary commodities, a percentage decline in their export earnings
> which might appear small arithmetically could cause grave damage.
> For example, a six per cent drop in their average export prices, were
> it to take place, would imply for the underdeveloped countries a
> decline in foreign exchange earnings equivalent to something like
> one-half of all official economic grants and loans currently received
> from abroad in a year. Recessions in activity in the industrial coun-
> tries have caused declines of this order of magnitude in the recent
> past. Concerted international action would therefore be required to
> prevent any such decline in the prices and incomes of the primary
> producing countries as a result of disarmament.

## A DISARMED WORLD

What would be the economic image of a disarmed world? Its
shape would largely depend on the alternative uses toward

which the resources released from armaments were directed. Many of the most urgent needs of mankind have so far remained unsatisfied because precious resources were turned to destructive purposes.

*Alternative uses for resources devoted to armaments.* The resources released from armaments can be used for many purposes, such as raising levels of personal consumption, expanding productive capacity, social investment, and aid to underdeveloped countries. These claims are not only interlinked—in the sense that an increase in one depends upon an increase in another—but they are also competing. While disarming, it would therefore be necessary for each country to establish a scale of priorities based on its needs and consistent with the possibilities of satisfying them.

Since social investments have often given way to the claims of military expenditures, it is of some relevance to give an idea of the wide scope that exists in this field. After thousands of years of cold and dreary winter, the arrival of springtime of mankind—a century of the machine age—has so far mainly helped raise levels of living only in the industrial countries. Most of mankind is still ill-fed, ill-clad, ill-housed, and illiterate. But even in the richest countries of the world, there are widespread deficiencies in capital for such social investment.

The National Planning Association estimated that to carry out the existing public programs of development and improvement in the United States, the present public expenditure of about $30 billion per year would have to be more than doubled —a vast sum indeed. Urban centers are expanding rapidly. In the Soviet Union, the housing problem remains acute. "The growth of the urban population in the Soviet Union during the past few years is considerably in excess of the estimates," said

Premier Khrushchev in his report to the twenty-second congress of the Communist party. The conditions of urban living, as reflected in the existence of slums, bad housing, poor community services, delinquency, paralysis of city traffic, and inadequate sanitation, are deteriorating.

The world's needs for development and conservation of natural resources are immense. It has been estimated for the United States that water-resource development alone would require federal expenditures amounting to nearly $55 billion up to 1980; nonfederal programs would need as much as $173 billion. Huge nature transforming projects in various parts of the world are awaiting execution. In the underdeveloped countries many important multipurpose schemes could be carried out if adequate resources were available.

Even in the richest countries, there is room for improvement of the medical and health services. In the rest of the world, they are simply inadequate. Mortality rates of infants and of pregnant women are high. Millions of people still suffer from diseases that would be easy to cure or to prevent if adequate resources were available. The age of enlightenment has so far seen its full fruition only in the industrially advanced countries, and even there scope for expansion of higher educational facilities is wide indeed. More than half the population in the rest of the world is still illiterate, unable to decipher the magic of the written word.

There are many other ventures that can be carried out adequately only through the international co-operation of many countries. Audacious undertakings remain today merely paper plans because of lack of mutual confidence among nations and availability of resources. A few of them may be cited: a worldwide network of meteorological stations, telecommunications, air transport; utilization of atomic energy for peaceful purposes; space research to widen the horizons of the universe within man's reach; exploration of the Arctic and Antarctic; control of desert locusts, which continue to devastate crops in Africa and western Asia, through the establishment of highly international brigades; research into the earth's interior; and, above all, joint programs to put an end as rapidly as possible to hunger and poverty in the industrially less developed countries.

Drawing pointed attention to the vast magnitude of the major needs of mankind that have so far remained unsatisfied, the United Nations experts concluded that "the resources freed by disarmament would not be large enough for the many claims upon them. . . . It seems abundantly clear that no country need fear a lack of useful employment opportunities for the resources that would become available to it through disarmament."

*International aid to developing countries.* Perhaps the most important advantage of disarmament would accrue to the developing countries. So far they have benefited only marginally from the vast advances in modern science and technology. Two-thirds of the world population in these countries produce only about one-fifth of the world output. Per-capita income for this overwhelming majority of mankind is only one-tenth of that in the industrial countries. International attention and growing concern for their poverty has so far done little to narrow the economic distance that separates the rich and poor countries. The rate of growth of per-capita output in the poor countries over the last twenty years has remained lower than in the rich ones.

To narrow this vast and growing gap, the growth rate of the poor economies has to be raised significantly above that of the rich ones. The United Nations experts emphasized that "the responsibility for initiation and intensification of development efforts will continue to lie entirely with the governments and peoples" of the underdeveloped countries. But many of these countries would be faced with grave shortages of foreign exchange if they were to embark on ambitious plans for raising the volume and the rate of capital formation in their economies.

The flow of foreign assistance to these countries can be increased manifold once the industrial countries have eliminated armament expenditure. The United Nations experts, however, warned that "because the competing claims in developed countries are also urgent, there is a serious possibility that the financial resources released by disarmament might be rapidly absorbed by purely national aims. It is therefore desirable that an appropriate proportion of these resources should be allocated to international aid in its various forms simultaneously with their use for domestic purposes."

The impact of a large increase in international aid (as a result of disarmament) to the developing countries may be illustrated by a hypothetical example. If the total capital flow from the industrial countries, both in the East and in the West, were to rise to $15 billion a year, this would amount to a little more than 1 per cent of their combined gross national product. It would be a small share of what they spend at present upon armaments. But this sum is nearly twice as high as the total volume of machinery and equipment that is being imported every year by all the underdeveloped countries. Even if half of this sum were to be spent exclusively on expanding the imports of machinery and equipment in these countries, it would form a basis for doubling the present level of investment.

The influence of such a rise in investment on the growth rate f the economy would perhaps be more than proportionate, since proper management of investment plans often yields a relatively higher growth rate per each additional unit of investment. But even doubling the growth rate would mean a rise rom the present rate of about 3 per cent to 6 or 7 per cent. With population increasing at about 2 per cent per year, the per-capita rate of growth would rise from just about 1 per cent o as high as 4 to 5 per cent. At this rate, per-capita output in these countries could rise sevenfold to tenfold in fifty years—or nearly equal to the present level in the industrial countries.

The diversion of even a small proportion of the resources devoted to war to assist the developing countries would provide the basis for a final solution of mankind's age-old affliction of squalor, poverty, want, and disease. The choice facing mankind is between half an hour of insanity and half a century of wise international co-operation.

# ⋑ PART III

# The Church's Ministry and the New Era

# 7

# LEISURE IN THE NEW ERA

### by Cameron P. Hall

## A CONSUMER-LEISURE ORIENTED SOCIETY

As a people we Americans have the capacity to provide for our needs; beyond that, we are satisfying a constantly expanding range of what we want. There is no limiting horizon to the volume of goods we can produce and the services we can provide. Such is our affluence.

Underlying this present and potential plenty is the fact that as a nation we have overcome the problem of production from a national viewpoint. This fact is on its way to becoming a truism. But this does not necessarily solve all our problems, even our "production" ones. Merely to stay where we have arrived, we will have to nourish our production processes with new investments, invigorate them with new inventions, and man them with newly trained workers and managers.

The present broad solution of production leads to a new plateau of equally pressing problems. Our affluent society is like a super-giant, king-sized supermarket. What shall—what should—we as consumers buy from its heavily stocked shelves? Also, the work day and work week become shorter, the number of holidays greater, the vacation period longer, and retirement earlier. To what use will we put this "free time"?

Underlying our production prowess is the machine. In terms of the volume of what is made and "gets done," not man but the machine is today's worker-producer. The machines which men invent are turning out consumer products in amount and variety far beyond anything men by themselves could do. Another way of putting this is that the output per hour of today's worker is six times that of his grandfather. Behold, for example, what has been happening "down on the farm." Technology has driven the horse off the farm, it has nearly dispensed with the horse's owner, the farmer himself! Because technology is so largely today's producer, the problem of production is essentially solved.

It should be noted that about one-fifth of the American people suffer from poverty. Does not this, it may be asked, show a lack of capacity to produce? On the contrary! It shows a failure of some people to obtain sufficient food, clothing, and adequate housing from our abundant production of goods. Our success in production makes poverty within the United States technically unnecessary. The poor among us are victims of our failure in distribution, not in production.

In passing, it may be pointed out that although we now live in an era of plenty, some of our thinking is geared to an era of scarcity. Many current economic theories took shape when production in the countryside and in the towns was far from being solved. But we continue to approach problems of today's relative plenty with ideas from yesterday's relative scarcity. For example, we try to solve our agricultural surplus by creating scarcity through taking acres out of production. At a time of global hunger, what the world needs is our surplus, not our scarcity! Although an approach from relative plenty would not bring an easy answer, at least it would be based on the realities of today's hunger.

As conventionally understood from the national viewpoint, the problem of producing has been essentially conquered. But this simple way of stating it can be misleading. We may be producing too many guns and not enough butter; too many pieces of jewelry and not enough schoolrooms. Certainly the ethical and social implications of this fact are of immediate and long-term importance. These point to such questions as: The production of *what* has been solved? of what goods and of what services? For what needs and for what wants may the production problem still be *unsolved?* These questions lead to central ethical issues in today's production problem.

These considerations are paramount for a people moving from a producer-worker to a consumer-leisure society. Our unprecedented affluence and productive know-how open for us the opportunity to shift our focus from "how much?" to "how worthy?"—from quantity to quality. Our material abundance consists of what are called "goods" and "services." Of their *quantity*, at hand and in prospect, there can be no doubt. But of their *quality*, in terms of what people need to become more human, there must be real misgivings. Within the wide range and the vast potential of human life, what areas do today's goods and services provide for, appeal to, or neglect?

We immediately confront a major difficulty in any sharp stress on worth or quality. We have to break out of our imprisonment by the meanings which these key words of economic activity—goods and services—have acquired. Let us now look at the limited meaning each has and the larger meaning each should take on.

In their origin, "goods" and "services" are related to the "good life"; they have an ethical parentage. But they have wandered far afield. They have become secularized. In modern technical and common usage, "goods" are equated with products that can be weighed and measured and counted; they are tangible and can be handled; they can fit into a money economy geared to private profit.

Production is intended to issue in these goods; "to be productive" is to be employed in making these goods: in mining, construction, farming, manufacturing. For example, to make military hardware which is designed solely to destroy people and what people need is to be "productive"; it is to produce "goods." By contrast, what an amateur painter creates for his own enjoyment and perhaps for the enjoyment of others does not come within the conventional usage of the term "goods." A consumer-leisure oriented society will require an enlargement of "productivity" to provide for needs and wants related to the quality of living.

The need also exists for an appraisal of the current meaning of the word "services." In today's vocabulary, "services" are primarily related to producing activities: transportation, finance, trade, public utilities, government. For convenience, then, let us call these "facilitating services," for directly or indirectly they help the productive process.

A mark of an affluent society is the growth of "personal services." These cater largely to the convenience, comfort, appearance, and pleasure of the individual and the family. Among these services are those provided by the beautician, gas station attendant, golf club professional, and the soda jerker. Of a different kind, but commonly included in personal services, are what are called "professional services" rendered by doctors, nurses, lawyers, and those in related occupations.

Some of these facilitating and personal services are indispensable; many are important; all contribute something. But together they do not measure the fullness of what "services" can provide in view of the capacity of a person to be a truly *human* being. And so, again for clarity, we add another category and include "enrichment services." The artist, the librarian, the musician, the educator, the philosopher, the clergyman, the counselor—these and similar persons provide enrichment services that add to the quality of living, in its individual and corporate aspects, with a directness and richness that are not found in the other needed services.

The foregoing has been written not to list or classify certain occupations, but to examine the main types of "services" as that term is or may be used today. What is the relevance of this brief analysis of the several types of services available and needed? Obviously, the facilitating services are not an immediate concern in our focus on the ethical implications of a consumer-leisure in contrast to a producer-worker oriented society. These services are imbedded in the process by which those goods are produced which are needed for the other kinds of services.

But the personal and enrichment services *are* related to the quality of living in a consumer-oriented society. What purposes are served by the many present and emerging personal services? What resources for individual and corporate living should be made available through still inadequately developed enrichment services? These latter questions bear upon the nature and promise of today's leisure, to which we now turn.

### LEISURE: TODAY AND TOMORROW

There is the familiar story of the man who dashed for a subway train "to save my having to wait three minutes for the next one." "What will you do with the three minutes you saved?" asked his friend.

*War, work, and leisure cultures.* Modern technology is essentially saving time in getting work done. What will we as a people do with the time thus saved? Some of it we will spend in adding to our goods and services. But not all! What will we do with the time which we do not choose to spend at work? is a critical question confronting us as a people.

It is a bewildering question. We are torn within ourselves by it. On the one hand, we would seek to reduce the work day and the work week because of the allurements of the consumer-leisure style of life. On the other hand, we are dependent on employment for financial security and status, and there is also, especially among Protestants, a cultural enshrinement of work as virtuous. The inner confusion is compounded by our not knowing what leisure is. Is its meaning to be found in freedom from work? in recreation? in idleness? in self-fulfillment? in contemplation? To equate leisure with "free time" leaves the big question unasked: Free for what?

Perhaps a partial answer to this inner bewilderment may be found in the lack of consensus about the nature and purpose of work. It has been observed that the terms "toil" and "labor" have been used as well as "work," each lifting out one aspect of the common experience: toil as painful, labor as arduous, and work as expenditure of energy.[1] If reflection on work, which is as old as mankind, still makes for varied understanding of its nature and purpose, there may be wisdom in not pushing too hard now for clear answers.

In its present form, leisure is a Johnny-come-lately on the human scene. In only a strictly limited sense can the Greeks be said to have articulated in theory and achieved leisure in practice. This leisure was enjoyed by but a fraction of the population; the rest were slaves who knew only toil, labor, and work— the ancient counterparts of our technological devices.

Today, in contrast, the use of leisure has wide practical consequences. This is now the problem and opportunity not of a class but of a people. This is a unique situation. Viewed broadly and with some oversimplification, all civilizations have been oriented either toward war and its preparation or toward work and its rewards (i.e., work for the many, rewards for the few). The dominant attitudes, social values, and political and economic forms throughout history have supported warfare or work.

Obviously, ours is a culture in which work and its rewards have held top priority. But today we are on the threshold of a transition undreamed of in scope. No other generation of men has stood or imagined standing where we now stand. Because of our science and technology, our society is increasingly capable of being organized around leisure rather than around work.

*Leisure for whom?* Because our newly acquired leisure grows out of modern technology, it has a distinctive character. Different groups are differently affected.

1. Managerial, professional, and educational groups: Although the level of expenditure in the leisure which they have is vastly higher, people in these categories probably work as

many hours today as their predecessors did some decades ago. "According to the Census Bureau, managers and proprietors work 53 hours a week. This does not include the work they carry home with them."[2] Teachers and lawyers with briefcases en route home give evidence of their long hours of work.

2. The "enforced leisure" class: The creation of additional jobs annually is not matching the combination of workers displaced by automation and new entrants (youth and women) into the work force. We even face the possibility that some who can and want to work may never work; these have been called the "liberated margin." That we may be moving in this direction is indicated in the following survey of unemployment trends:

. . . from the three previous slumps (1949, 1954, 1958) of the past nine years . . . the upturns have been getting weaker and shorter in duration. . . . Unemployment has moved up after each slump, in steady succession, and the unemployment level, now, is greater than at the start of any previous postwar economic decline. The unemployment rate has been 5 per cent or more for the past 57 consecutive months, except February 1960.[3]

3. Homemakers: Home appliances, bakeries, laundries, and other modern innovations have measurably increased the work capability of wives and mothers. These persons now have more free hours. How do they dispose of this newly acquired time free from homework? There is little reliable information. Certainly some are found in other groups listed here; others *by choice* become part-time workers; still others engage in the manifold forms of free-time activities.

4. Retired persons: "Not working is the fastest growing of all leisure occupations in the United States today. The number of non-workers has roughly doubled in the past decade and might

well double again by 1970." [4] The Social Security Administration has estimated that by 1970 the number of Americans receiving payments through Old Age and Survivors Insurance will rise to nineteen million, which will represent about 80 per cent of all people in the sixty-five and over age bracket.

5. Those with additional leisure: The following is from a condensation of an article in the *Monthly Labor Review*, issued by the U.S. Department of Labor:

Essentially the increase in leisure time in 1960 over 1940 consists of the following:

|  | Hours per year per full-time employed person |
|---|---|
| 1½ hours less in the workweek | 75 |
| 6 days more paid vacation | 48 |
| 4 days more paid holidays | 32 |
| Total | 155 |

For the economy as a whole, this additional leisure time amounts to over 10 billion hours.

In summary of the foregoing, it becomes apparent that the amount of time now free from work is not easily determined. This is not only a matter of statistics; it is mainly one of definition, or more accurately, of a state of mind. Should time spent in daily commuting to and from work be counted a part of, or apart from, work? Again, should time spent by a young executive in painting his suburban home be put on the work or the leisure side of his time sheet? Different people, different answers!

These factors suggest the need for some reticence in assuming complete knowledge of just how much leisure time people have and are using. But this does not detract from what is of vast significance for this generation: We have reached a technological development by which we can increase our goods and services even while we increase our time away from work. We are becoming a consumer-leisure based society. This is true today to such an extent that we are aware of, and appalled at, both the threat and the promise in the use to which we put our leisure time.

One mark of a leisure society is the leap forward in the number and volume of leisure-time industries. This should not be surprising: leisure stimulates consumption of many kinds of goods and services. We travel in the family car, and motels spring up; we go in for sports, and bowling alleys are built; we stay indoors, and TV sets become a necessity; we go outdoors, and hunting licenses, swimming pools, and motorboats multiply. Leisure time opens employment doors for new service occupations. What is leisure for some requires work by others.

A second mark of a leisure society is more subtle, but perhaps more important. Paul's dictum that "if a man does not work neither shall he eat" no longer holds sway as it once did. For *nonwork* as well as work has become an acknowledged basis for being paid an income. One of the social values in a society which is both affluent and democratic is that, under certain conditions, by not working one "earns" a livelihood. Retirement under Social Security is a notable example; so are unemployment compensation and industry S.U.B. (supplementary unemployment benefit) plans. These provide incomes not as a matter of charity, but of justice. They show that the concept of nonwork has become an accepted and formative concept in public and private policy.

*Our inherited work-based culture.* As our society steadily makes the transition from work-based to leisure-based, work may eventually become viewed as time off from leisure. But that is many decades away. In the meantime this transition period will be under the value system of our inherited work-based culture. Leisure will be seen and grasped as "free time," time free from work. Because work traditionally has ruled men's daily routine, leisure may easily appeal to many people as an escape from having to work, to others as the opposite of work, and to still others as compensation for having to work. Hence it will prove difficult to see what leisure is in its own right and what "goods" and "services" are appropriate to it.

There is evidence of this limited way of thinking of "leisure" merely as time freed from work. Leisure is widely seen quantitatively and hence superficially: it is hours or days off from work. Again, leisure is seen negatively, and hence uncreatively: it is freedom *not to be* (a worker) rather than freedom *to be* (a whole man).

The long work-production shadow further darkens our understanding of how to enter fruitfully into the newly glimpsed leisure era that beckons us. For multitudes, work is equated with the necessity of being on time and not quitting ahead of time, the demands of the rhythm of the machine, the pressure of the deadline, the authority of one's employer, immediate or remote, and the deep emotional dependence upon employment for security and status. When the shorter work week or the longer paid vacation comes, leisure tends to take the shape of freedom from responsibility, from necessity, from discipline. If leisure is time free from work, and work has been experienced as essentially external discipline and control, then whatever else it may be, leisure is equated with living in freedom. And freedom without responsibility borders upon license.

Again, what men have been accustomed to work for will

affect how they use their leisure. In our business, consumer-active society, men work in large measure to gain money or to qualify for credit, in order to buy material things or semiluxury services. One does not deny the place of a valid materialism when one points to today's materialism as being excessive. What more likely, then, than that modern man will spend his time free from work centering on what he has worked to produce: material things. Man as consumer may come to see the meaning of his leisure in the use ("enjoyment") of the product of man as worker: material goods!

*Our Puritan and biblical heritage.* As is invariably pointed out in a discussion of this kind, our Puritan heritage is still a living, although waning, force. The Puritan tended to be afraid of idleness. Work was not only a positive good; it was a lid upon the sins that come in when work goes out. The Puritan ethic was an ethic of work; its virtues were those related to work and to the enhancement of the rewards that come from work.

In this there was nothing inherently wrong. In the seventeenth century this ethic of work was sorely needed, and it has served the Western world well since then. What was wrong was that this ethic of work all but stood alone. It was not balanced with an ethic of leisure and with its attendant virtues related to contemplation, artistic creativity, and intellectual ferment.

The result was what one would expect: a culture that magnifies "doing," and equates it with "getting things done" and made. What has been a producer-active culture has now become a consumer-active culture. Will it emerge into a leisure-active one? And if so, will this be "leisure"?

We need to bring to leisure the same seriousness that the Puritans brought to work, but with a new insight into the nature of time. In our work-producer based society, the prevailing view of time is quite rudimentary. It is "spatialized," measured by the time clock or fiscal year; it is "localized," placed in what is turned out or by what is earned. But there is as well a qualitative dimension to time, to which the work-virtuous Puritan was blind. This dimension is unrelated to meeting a deadline or reaching a measured output. In this non-Puritan aspect of time lies its prime meaning for leisure.

Hebrew society was work-high and leisure-low in its awareness and value system. A standard concordance shows about 458 references in the Bible to "work" and its compounds ("workman," "worker," etc.), while to leisure there is but a single reference; to "idle" or "idleness" there are ten. A ratio of 458 to 11 represents a vast difference! It is to be expected, then, that, as Canon Alan Richardson writes, "The Bible knows nothing of a 'problem of leisure.' No such problem had in fact arisen in the stage of social evolution which had been reached in biblical times. . . . The general standpoint of the Bible is that it is 'folly' (i.e. sinful) to be idle between daybreak and sunset. Hence we must not expect to derive from the Bible any explicit guidance upon the right use of leisure." [5]

No "explicit guidance," to be sure, but nevertheless the Bible is not without some kind of guidance, for work and leisure are both part of life. Indeed, in the fourth of the Ten Commandments, time free from work is enjoined upon men. That the minimum time possible—one day out of seven—is allotted to "rest" has no special significance. In the development of the worker-producer society which existed in biblical times, a ratio of 1 to 6 is to be expected. In a consumer-leisure society the ratio will be closer, even to the point where it may become six days of leisure to one of work!

It should be noted—even stressed—that this commandment does not give merely a negative view of the Sabbath, as freedom or rest from work. Its main thrust is for such use of that freedom as will build up the spiritual aspect of life. Obviously the Church of today is challenged to make clear that the gospel is as relevant to men with time free from work as it is to men burdened with toil.

*Leisure as an aspect of creation.* God as creator has been seen in too restricted a light by many men. He created and sustains the seas and earth and air in which lie the resources for man's material well-being. Man as worker, and increasingly through technology, joins with God in bringing these resources "into production" for human needs and wants. Not only "the earth," but "the fullness thereof" is the Lord's (Ps. 24:1). Because through science men have come to know so much about the earth and through technology have gained the means to turn to human usefulness its resources, the earth now yields an abundance ("fullness") of *both* the fruits of work and time off from work. Leisure as a fact has its source in "the earth and the fullness thereof," of which God is the creator.

Beyond the fact lies its promise. God's creative touch is upon the possibilities for personhood to which leisure can be put. People are a part of God's creation, and men must be seen as made for leisure as our present cultural orientation sees them made for work. God works *through men* to produce what can be weighed or measured, bought or sold; he works as well *within men* to bring out what is latent in their mind, their sensibilities, their imagination. Some of God's work within men can be fostered by men's work experience; more of it waits upon constructive leisure. God as creator reveals his handiwork in literature, music, the arts, social relationships, and contemplation and reflection. These are as "productive" as employment in the auto industry or in the wall-to-wall carpet business.

*The opportunity to become more fully human.* For the Puritans, time was too important to be used casually or blindly. It was to be taken seriously and responsibly. In this we can learn from them. Their error lay in viewing too narrowly the uses to which men can put time. There is a wider choice than between time-at-work and time-in-idleness. Men can choose time-in-fruitful-leisure.

In our traditional work-production culture, the Christian Church has tended to relate stewardship primarily to spending one's means; its concern with spending time was with time at church. But in our emerging consumption-leisure oriented culture, the stewardship of time must be expanded: Spending time free from work must be treated as responsibly as spending income from work.

If, as is generally acknowledged to be the case, leisure is sought by many as an escape from the boredom and meaninglessness of work today, then whither lies escape if leisure itself yields boredom and meaninglessness? Some people are so unprepared for leisure that they enter upon it at its lower levels. Others start with some interest or purpose which proves too narrow to be sustained. For still others, "adult playthings," distractions, and activities for activities' sake seem to satisfy and for a while may even cover up the fact that the need is no longer being met. Others, however, show they have the secret or the know-how to find where the secret lies for fruitful leisure.

Any generation is doomed to boredom with leisure if it holds to our inherited view of what "to be productive" means, and of what our "needs" and "wants" are. The appeal of modern business to people as buyers generally sells short what people are and can become. Buyers also have a responsibility. Beyond their needs for food, clothing, shelter, and medical care, today's consumer-demands upon our technological productivity cater to only a fraction of our really *human* needs and wants.

Leisure means the opportunity to become more fully human than work by itself enables man to be. It is the door to growth into the whole man, which is what God created men to be. Someone has said that the mind is the most underdeveloped area in the world today. Another has pointed to the frontiers of artistic interest and expression that beckon. There is excitement of the imagination and spirit in creative activity of many kinds which makes much of Madison Avenue's consumer-stimulating devices seem pale and wan.

If the coming era of leisure is not based on the search and provision for growth into greater humanness, then its meaninglessness could be worse than no leisure. But this need not be. It is not a matter of a person becoming a different kind of person, but rather that he become a whole person.

*From marginal to fuller citizenship.* The use which a person makes of his leisure is his individual responsibility. But the fact that he has leisure is due to society, for leisure is a social product. It comes out of the way we have lived and worked together as a people over many generations. It is to be used, therefore, with a sense of social responsibility.

Leisure must be used with a sense of historic urgency, as well. It may be argued that but for the advent of the era of new leisure, our democratic institutions might become seriously impaired, our urban communities might be unsuited to serve people, and our nation's leadership in the free world might falter. Put another way, marginal-time citizenship is not enough.

Our complex society at home and today's interdependent world require new levels of citizen competence. Democracy needs more time from its citizens, and this is now at hand.

The time free from work can result in a more informed and participating body of citizens. The earlier minimum leisure joined to today's complex social problems might be used to justify handing these problems over to the expert, the professional, the politician. But more time is now available for us to become qualified amateurs in regard to the demands of citizenship. When employment restricts a people's free time, there may be little grass-roots participation in public affairs. But a socially responsible approach to the use of leisure should now result in more than marginal time spent in such participation by a larger number of citizens.

This increased citizen participation should include efforts for vastly expanded facilities for leisure time. Today's work-producer society is bare of all but the most rudimentary resources which a consumer-leisure oriented society will require and can afford if its leisure, in turn, is to be oriented toward quality of living.

Provision of these resources is largely a responsibility of society. For the task of moving into an era of fruitful leisure cannot be put upon the individual alone. Society, not the individual, can provide an environment equipped to excite the imagination with leisure's possibilities, to develop attitudes and skills that leisure needs, to enlarge people's range of interests, and to give play to their capacity for growth. Such aids include turning federal and state lands into wildernesses, forests, and parks; urban planning that provides not only for housing and transportation, but for adequate open spaces; varied formal and informal educational opportunities; TV programs not based on success in selling the products of the sponsor; civic art and music centers; public golf courses, tennis courts, other recreational areas, and libraries and museums. Achieving a society of an expanding population moving into an expanding freedom from work is the continuing task of society itself. This is essentially a civic matter: citizens co-operating in voluntary groups, including churches, and also through all levels of government.

# 8

## STEWARDSHIP: PRIVATE AND PUBLIC

### by Ross M. Robertson

For more than a century American religious bodies—Roman Catholic, Protestant, and Jewish—have been a major force for the enrichment of life and the improvement of welfare. Committed churchmen of whatever faith have time and again inquired whether this influence grows or declines, continually reassessing the contribution of religious groups to the good life. But in recent years their concern has deepened, for it superficially appears that the welfare state, on the one hand, and the "suburban captivity" of the churches, on the other, have weakened the bonds between religion and society.

Just a little more than fifty years ago the churches began on a scale never previously attempted to relieve the strains and tensions of their members and the nonmembers to whom they minister. Furthermore, since governmental welfare expenditures began their upsurge in the 1930s, religious bodies have held their own in relative importance, and this despite the failure of their memberships to contribute financially at anything like rates indicated by both Christian and Jewish precepts. It is equally true, however, that since 1926 the churches have made no spectacular gains as welfare organizations, and while there is little evidence of lessening influence neither is there any indication of a return to religion that manifests itself in substantially increasing proportions of income going to religious institutions.

This chapter has a twofold aim: to assess the relative importance of the churches as contributors to welfare and to consider their probable future role in providing for human needs. We begin by estimating expenditures of religious bodies over the past two generations both for their self-perpetuation and for missions and other benevolences. We then examine historic changes in social welfare programs under public programs, observing how total expenditures have changed both as a percentage of gross national product and as a percentage of all government expenditures. At the end of the chapter we suggest the way in which Christians and Jews must meet the challenge of rapid social and economic change, not by endlessly passing on to government further responsibilities, but by permanently assuming the direct burden of certain kinds of welfare work.

## I

Statistics of both church membership and church finances are notoriously inaccurate. Catholics and Jews are reluctant to divulge information. The major Protestant denominations are free enough with their figures, but their data-collecting processes are inaccurate, and many smaller denominations simply do not respond to questionnaires. Moreover, the basis of reporting information has changed over the years, and even today there is lack of agreement on certain concepts.[1] Nevertheless, data are available that may be considered reliable enough for purposes of comparison and generalization; the reader is simply cautioned that many of the quantitative relationships to be described should be accepted as no more than careful estimates.

Any reckoning of the importance of the churches as welfare institutions must begin with some notice of changes in membership, for in one sense Christians and Jews may be thought of as large mutual-aid groups. Over the long pull, gains in membership have been impressive. In 1800, nominal members of religious bodies probably numbered between 5 and 10 per cent of the population, and as late as the years between 1850 and 1890, church membership fluctuated in the neighborhood of 20 per cent of the population. From something more than one-third of the population in 1900, membership has soared to 63 per cent in 1960.

Clergy and laity alike have enthusiastically read into these figures optimistic portents. In a sense, the ratios of membership to total population somewhat understate people's subjective sense of religious affiliation. In March, 1957, the U.S. Bureau of the Census asked, "What is your religion?" in a sample survey, and more than 97 per cent of persons fourteen or older reported a religious connection. But if this figure means anything, it is only that less than 3 per cent of the population consider themselves atheist. For that matter, much of the actual membership on church and synagogue rolls is dead wood, though sample surveys indicate an astonishingly high percentage of church attendance at one time or another during the year.

More important for present purposes is the fact that the percentage of the adult population actually enrolled as church members has been approximately stable for at least two generations. Writing in the early 1930s on the basis of fairly recent official census data, C. Luther Fry observed: "Government figures show that the total number of church members in the United States has been growing at virtually the same rate as the population. In 1926, as well as in 1916 and 1906, the persons thirteen years of age and over listed on the membership rolls of the churches were equivalent to 55 per cent of the total number of persons of that age in the population." [2] It is a reasonable estimate that the percentage of persons thirteen years of age and over currently listed on membership rolls of churches is still about equal to 55 per cent of that age group in the total population, for Roman Catholics and certain Protestant denominations, notably Lutherans and Episcopalians, count baptized persons as members. In other words, the churches seem to have had about the same basic hold on people for the past fifty years, and we delude ourselves if we interpret current membership figures as signifying a renewed religious life in America.

We must now inquire how this approximately stable proportion of the adult population has contributed to church support. At first glance the figures are reassuring. According to a widely accepted estimate of expenditures by religious organizations, giving to the churches amounted to $4.43 billion in 1961. [3] This estimate is almost certainly somewhat short of the actual figure, for it unquestionably underestimates the contributions of Roman Catholics. Alfred de Grazia and Ted Gurr feel that the American Association of Fund-Raising Counsel estimate of $3.9 billion for 1959 was short by a little over a billion dollars, and the 1961 estimate may well be low by $1.25 billion or more. [4] For the sake of uniformity we may stick with the AAFRC estimate, but the fact that it underestimates actual giving should be kept in mind.

Two significant historical comparisons are possible. In the first place, the amount of giving to the churches has for a long time remained astonishingly close to 1 per cent of the national income. Estimated church expenditures for 1926 were $840 million, almost exactly 1 per cent of the national income for that year. Ten years earlier outlays had been in the neighborhood of $350 million, something under 1 per cent of national income for 1916.[5] Observers of the late 1920s and early 1930s thought this ten-year increase in giving as a percentage of the national income significant, but it is by no means certain that the change was outside the limits of statistical error. Similarly, the last thirty-five years may have witnessed a slight upward trend in the propensity of members of religious bodies to give to their organizations. The AAFRC estimate of $4.43 billion of church expenditures for 1961 was remarkably close to that year's national income of $428 billion. If, on the other hand, we agree that AAFRC estimates understate Roman Catholic expenditures, consequently estimating total outlays for 1961 to be somewhat over $5.5 billion, church expenditures for that year amounted to a little more than 1¼ per cent of the national income.

During the past two generations have there been any demonstrable changes in the way religious bodies spend their income? Once again available data suggests a remarkable stability of attitudes. The *Census of Religious Bodies* asked reporting churches to separate expenditures for 1926 into two parts: (1) current expenditures and improvements and (2) sums spent for benevolences and missions. Responses indicated that eighty cents of every dollar went for local self-support and twenty cents was contributed to works outside local units. More than a generation later the same 80-20 breakdown still applies and seems to be consistently maintained in successive annual estimates.[6]

The fact that four-fifths or more of the funds raised by churches are spent on support of local units will astonish no one with experience at parochial levels. The loyalties of Christians and Jews are clearly to church and synagogue; it is in the Hebrew-Christian tradition that social responsibility should manifest itself first in concern for neighbor. Moreover, there is really no substitute for the welfare services performed by members of a congregational family, with their unique quality of intimacy that gives the church its permanent role in welfare work. There is at the same time a danger, one that grows no less serious as years go by, that churches everywhere will become what many already are—social clubs that provide warm meeting places, peripheral social activities, and precious little more.

Although the chief welfare role of religious bodies is largely through congregational units, social concern is manifested in other ways requiring financial contribution over and above amounts indicated by the foregoing estimates. Unfortunately, Protestant, Catholic, and Jewish welfare organizations fall into no simple, orderly classifications, and institutional details are beyond the scope of this chapter.[7] Nonetheless, there would probably be substantial agreement on the following generalizations.

Protestant social services constitute a heterogeneous category of good works characterized by noble motivation and no clear principles of operation. These services are not directed toward any particular Protestant objectives; indeed, Protestants have little objection to the secularization of welfare institutions largely because there are few denominational differences over what constitutes a "proper" solution of human problems. As one writer has put it,

When . . . the majority of the religious population belongs to communions which differ in relatively inconspicuous ways, the differences between the social ideals or standards of the community as a whole are usually not great. Thus Protestants adjusted themselves to the passing over of social work to secular, nonsectarian auspices, in the same fashion as they did with respect to the secularization of education.[8]

The most recent comprehensive information about Protestant social efforts is furnished by a National Council of Churches survey made in 1954. In the mid-1950s, Protestants had about four thousand closely related health and welfare agencies that served seventeen million people annually and spent over a billion dollars on current expenses. Employing nearly a quarter of a million workers, these agencies utilized the services of many technically and professionally trained personnel, including physicians, nurses, and social workers. These Protestant agencies chiefly provided for child care, homes and services for the aged, hospitalization, pastoral and psychiatric counseling, overseas relief and reconstruction, family case work, and city missions. Although most Protestant health and welfare organizations have strong ties to church organizations, church connection does not imply extensive church financial support. Indeed, if we include hospitals, which earn much of their income, less than 1 per cent of the support of these church-related agencies comes from religious groups; excluding hospitals, direct church support of these agencies amounted to less than one-sixth of their total income.

The welfare concern of the Roman Catholic Church is probably more intense than that of Protestants taken as a whole. Catholics are scarcely more inclined to describe their activities than to furnish estimates of their financial contributions. It is nevertheless clear that through diocesan agencies, service programs, and religious orders, the Roman Church is a major force in social work. On the assumption that educational outlays are a part of social welfare expenditures in the broadest sense, the parochial school system of the Catholic Church would add an impressive amount to the total.

Although the Catholic parish undertakes primary responsibility for its own people, social services have developed largely on the diocesan level. They are centered in Catholic Charities, an agency of the bishop ordinarily directed by a priest trained in social work. In 1959, there were 340 diocesan and branch agencies of Catholic Charities in the United States. These organizations provided much the same type of service rendered by the Protestant welfare agencies, but in addition to direct jurisdiction over service and assistance programs, diocesan agencies fulfill a planning and co-ordinating role usually lacking in Protestant efforts. It is probably not unfair to say that Catholic social workers are less likely to be embarrassed by using religion as a tool in their daily tasks and that Catholics are less likely than Protestants to favor the continuing secularization of welfare services. It also seems a fair judgment that Catholics make greater proportionate contributions to the total expenses of Catholic Charities than do Protestants to their welfare agencies.

Of the three major religious groups, Jews probably have the most effective organization for ministering to their own coreligionists. Jews live in cities, 90 per cent of the more than five million Jews in the United States residing in ninety-four urban areas, so that the social work of Jewish congregations has a narrow focus. Like Christians, Jews perform many welfare functions through the local unit—temple or synagogue—but in the late 1950s there were some 290 federations, welfare funds, and community councils associated with the Council of Jewish Federations and Welfare Funds. Of an estimated $170 million contributed in 1956 to local Jewish health and welfare services, 40 per cent came from Jewish philanthropy, a larger proportion than Christians gave. Jews are also generous in the support of education, and they provide relatively greater financial support for national and international programs than do their Christian brethren. For understandable reasons, their good works have a remarkably secular nature, largely for the reason that the American Jewish community is as much social and cultural as religious.

In summary, the welfare contribution of religious bodies is substantial indeed. Besides direct denominational support of church memberships, large sums are raised each year in support of church-related welfare programs. A relatively small proportion of this support comes directly in the form of religious giving, but the funds raised from all sources, including charges for some services, presently exceed $2 billion per annum. Such outlays mark a tremendous gain over those made before the turn of the twentieth century, for the notion that the churches at one time provided the bulk of welfare services has no basis in fact.[9] Both absolutely and relatively, churches and church-related agencies unquestionably contribute more to human welfare today than they did a generation ago and incomparably more than they did two generations ago.

The fact remains that there has not been a verifiable upward trend in the percentage of income going directly to religious bodies. At the very outside, a shift has occurred in the proportion of national income going to charitable contributions of from ¾ of 1 per cent in 1916 to 1¼ per cent in the early 1960s. If these figures actually mark a trend, the churches can look toward a level of giving approaching 2 per cent of the national income in another fifty years or so. A more conservative, and probably more realistic, estimate is that formal giving each year will hover slightly above 1 per cent of the national income and that giving to religious organizations will increase about as the national income increases.

II

Any discussion of the social role of the churches must sooner or later consider the question whether their work is being superseded by publicly supported welfare services. On the basis of intuition and casual observation we are likely to jump to the conclusion that only highly specialized functions remain to churches and other private groups.

Examination of the data reveals relationships that do not fit this prejudgment. It is true that public outlays on welfare are much greater today than they were before the Great Depression. Indeed, the shabby treatment accorded unfortunates and the unwillingness of Americans to undertake social insurance programs was nothing short of disgraceful in the years before 1933.

We have only estimates of social welfare expenditures before the beginning of major federal programs in the 1930s, but even with considerable allowance for error the meager commitment of Americans is plain enough. In 1890, total social welfare expenditures are estimated at $318 million or 2.4 per cent of the gross national product. By 1913, the figure was a billion dollars or 2.8 per cent of the gross national product, and by 1929 it had risen to $4.3 billion or 4.1 per cent of the gross national product.[10] Included in the categories of social welfare expenditures are all social insurance programs, public aid, health and medical programs, vocational rehabilitation, institutional care, school lunch programs, child welfare, education, and public housing.[11] Although these sums were a small proportion of GNP, they constituted 38 per cent, 34 per cent, and 42 per cent of total government expenditures in the years 1890, 1913, and 1929.

The common impression that the "welfare state" began in the 1930s is borne out by the figures. Social welfare programs in 1935 required a $6.7 billion outlay, 9.8 per cent of that year's GNP and a little more than half of government expenditures at all levels and for all purposes. During World War II these expenditures fell both absolutely and relatively, amounting to just over $7 billion in 1944, a substantial drop from the 1939 prewar peak of $9.6 billion. Welfare expenditures in 1944 were only 3.5 per cent of GNP and less than 7 per cent of total government expenditures.

Since the end of World War II social welfare expenditures have steadily risen, amounting to $52 billion in 1960 and an estimated $58 billion in 1961. This increase is largely accounted for by a steady rise in the total of social insurance outlays, particularly old-age and survivors insurance, and by educational expenditures, which rival those of social insurance as the most rapidly burgeoning category of welfare expenditures. Actually, public aid in the form of old-age assistance, aid to dependent children, aid to the blind, etc., plus work programs and other emergency-aid programs presently account for only a small proportion of social welfare expenditures, in 1961 amounting to about what they were in the depression years of the 1930s. During the 1950s social welfare expenditures varied from about 8.5 per cent to 10.7 per cent of the gross national product and throughout the decade constituted a little more than one-third of all government expenditures.

Contrary to a common impression, total expenditures of the federal government on social welfare are consistently less by several billion dollars a year than total state and local expenditures. The gap may be narrowing; nevertheless, the welfare state, if indeed it is upon us, is more responsive to local needs and susceptible of closer local supervision than is generally supposed. During the past few years social welfare expenditures as a percentage of the gross national product have moved up to approximately 11.5 per cent. Before 1960, expenditures of this type for some time held just under 25 per cent of all federal expenditures, but in the past two years they have crept up to 28 per cent or thereabouts. In recent years welfare expenditures have consistently amounted to approximately 60 per cent of all state and local expenditures. Again we must remind ourselves that the educational component of this series is large, particularly so for state and local governments. It is nevertheless significant that welfare still remains a matter of predominantly local concern.

## III

Two major conclusions emerge from the foregoing discussion. First, and contrary to a widespread opinion, the relative importance of the church's ministry to human needs is not declining. Beginning in the 1920s, the churches began to make a stronger commitment to welfare outlays than they had ever made before, and it is my judgment that for more than a generation the churches have maintained this commitment and probably increased it slightly.

There are two reasons for being hopeful about a continuing trend toward even greater responsibility on the part of religious bodies. For one thing, there is a growing propensity on the part of people everywhere to show more concern for human welfare. I have the impression that Americans were demonstrating this concern even before the revolution of the 1930s; over the long pull we have grown in willingness to live in love and charity with our neighbors. But even if fallible human beings had shown no improving disposition to relieve the cares of the world, the necessity would have been forced on them. For let us make no mistake about it! The revolution that is going on all over the globe is very largely a demand by poverty-ridden people for a more equitable income of this world's goods and services.

But there is another reason for thinking that, at least in the United States, private contributions to welfare will increase in greater proportion than incomes as a whole. Here we come to a fact of life that some people, notably clergy, recognize only reluctantly. Giving (philanthropy) is a luxury; giving, like saving, can be enjoyed chiefly by those who can afford it. Anyone who doubts this fact need only look at the income-tax deductions of individuals on account of philanthropic contributions. In 1958, for example, individuals with adjusted gross incomes of between $5,000 and $10,000 made philanthropic contributions equal to 3.52 per cent of their income. Individuals with incomes of between $100,000 and $500,000 contributed 7.73 per cent of their incomes, and those with a million dollars and more of income contributed nearly 17 per cent. As the years go on, more and more Americans move into upper income brackets; for this reason alone there will be a tendency for the percentage of giving to philanthropic causes to rise.

The second major conclusion to be reached from the foregoing analysis is that public expenditures for welfare are not growing as rapidly as is commonly believed. To put the matter another way, the data do not suggest that public welfare expenditures are swamping private expenditures in their total impact. There is no guarantee that this relationship will always hold; increased requirements for old-age benefits, for aid to the urban poor, and for education may raise substantially the *proportion* of the gross national product spent on these services. Actually, the health of the American economy will pretty well determine this outcome. If the economy performs at something like its vast potential, welfare expenditures will be a proportionately smaller charge on the gross product than if the economy persistently flags.

So far, so good. From the standpoint of (*a*) generosity and (*b*) ability to contribute, it looks as though the churches will maintain and probably increase their relative commitment. But what of the *demand* for the traditional welfare services of religious groups? We hear of late so much foolishness about the contemporary "affluent society" that we are likely to conclude the problem of poverty has been solved.[12] It is very much with us, of course, and will never go away. Even the least perceptive person need only look at American scenes of urban blight and agricultural decline to know that many, many people are by no means affluent. What our eyes tell us, statistical evidence confirms. In the relative prosperity of late 1962 the U.S. Department of Agriculture was giving surplus food to six million needy recipients. To take another figure: in 1960, 2.3 million multiple-person families and 2.1 million unattached individuals had incomes of less than $2,000; a frightening 10.4 million multiple-person families and almost 4 million unattached individuals had incomes of less than $6,000. These are the poor who live in substandard housing, who eat bad diets, and who have little hope of bettering their lot because they are for the most part the old and the uneducated. It is clear that for a long time to come these unfortunates will need help wherever they can find it.

In what ways should Christians and Jews show their concern? We often hear the remark that the church's role in welfare matters has traditionally been a "pioneering" one, that it should be the proper function of religious groups to allocate their scarce resources in ways that break new paths. This view has merit, though in its customary formulation it sometimes sounds like an excuse for not making adequate outlays along traditional lines. It is nevertheless undebatable that the churches will gain their greatest total effect in alleviating distress by planning a careful strategy in the war against human want.

I leave it to experts in these matters to devise such a strategy. I can speak only from narrow personal experience, and I am never sure that what my coreligionists and I have done is really worth the candle. I may say, for what it is worth, that we in the Episcopal Diocese of Indianapolis have based our social-welfare strategy on two fundamental principles. First, we are providing adequate physical facilities, located in the central city, for a counseling service that ranges from simple pastoral advice to professional psychiatric counseling. Adequate facilities, where clergy and concerned laymen in various fields of specialty can serve anyone in need, pay good dividends; for the contribution of personal talent is a part of stewardship, and the churches can lever the force of their ministry by serving as an intermediary for those who give of themselves. Second, in a world where open country and natural beauty are rapidly becoming a scarce commodity we have chosen to invest in land and facilities that will provide a refuge for young people and a place of retreat for old. Per dollar invested the churches get perhaps as much return from this kind of facility as any other.

These two types of investment are within the means of regional and even parochial groups. To them must be added a third that will ordinarily have to be financed by national organizations—expenditures on education. When all is said and done, increasing the productivity of people through education is the most important contribution to be made toward improving the quality of human life. Only the Roman Catholics contribute in anything like full measure to education. Protestant contributions are so meager as to be scandalous, denominational support of 247 church-related and church-controlled Protestant colleges receiving less than $20 million for current annual operating expenses in the mid-1950s. Protestants and Jews should concentrate on filling in some of the educational gaps in their society, possibly by sponsoring vocational educational facilities for young people who presently leave the inadequate curricula of our high schools and drift into unemployment and delinquency.

I leave it to my friends in clergy to set standards of stewardship in a day when, as tax-paying citizens, church members are required to pay substantial amounts for public support of welfare projects. It is naïve to suppose that many Christians and Jews will give a tithe, whether of the old-fashioned or "modern" variety. Giving must always be a matter of conscience, and personal standards of giving will inevitably be related to contributions of time and talent, on the one hand, and to personal obligations, on the other. The notion of giving as a response to God's gifts loses meaning when giving becomes perfunctory and mechanical—dues paid for the privilege of belonging to the club.

It is nonetheless true that church members do not for the most part lend financial support to their group efforts that even a half-hearted commitment would suggest. Orthodox Protestants are notorious in this regard, denominations with the highest incomes per capita ordinarily ranking well down in the published lists of per-capita giving. When Episcopalians, Presbyterians, Methodists, Baptists, and other members of the standard denominations of Protestantism begin to contribute at something like levels suggested by their professions of faith, the churches will become a social force to be reckoned with. Meantime, the cause is far from hopeless, and there is even some ground for cautious optimism. The work of the churches has an astonishing vitality.

## 9 ∻

# THE RECOVERY OF MINISTRY IN THE NEW ERA

### ∻ by Franklin H. Littell

In the rapid transformation of the United States from a rural people to an industrial society, a change which has been completed during the lifetime of the older communicants of our parishes, the rise of the Giant City (megalopolis) has come to be of marked importance. In 1890, 83 per cent of the American people still lived on farms or in rural villages. Today, over 25 per cent live in the twelve largest metropolitan areas and over 50 per cent are concentrated in 220 counties (with the rest in 2,800 counties). Eighty per cent of the population resides within twenty-five miles of cities of at least 25,000. The trend continues, and it is predicted that in the next decade there will emerge giant cities stretching from Arlington, Virginia, to Melrose, Massachusetts; from Akron to Toledo, Ohio; from Windsor, Ontario, to Lansing, Michigan; from Gary, Indiana, to Port Washington, Wisconsin; from San Diego to Santa Barbara, California. In this situation many of the institutions controlling social existence, developed under the conditions of rural neighborhoods, have become obsolete. As will be seen, the churches share their proportion of the institutional obsolescence.

The backwardness of some institutions, and the legal provisions covering them, is sometimes so great as to work great cruelty and injustice against whole sections of the American people. In the political sphere, this can be illustrated by the growing number of "rotten boroughs" which exercise—particularly at county level, but also in the malapportionment of representation in state legislatures—legal influence all out of proportion to their importance. As in England before the Great Reform Bill of 1832, many major political bodies in the United States are corruptly and immorally manipulated by machines which survive at the state level by controlling remote remnants of a few hundreds, while millions in the large cities are virtually disfranchised. The "county unit system" in some southern states has come to symbolize the lagging hostility to true and just representation, but conditions in New York state, Michigan, Iowa, and other northern states are little better. The tension existing between some state machines and the federal government, so dangerous to public order and civic morale, is to no small degree due to the fact that reapportionment of the House of Representatives is required by law after each census, whereas many states—often in open defiance of their own constitutions—have failed to realign representation for one, two, and even three generations. The decision of the U.S. Supreme Court in the Tennessee Case (June, 1962) points toward rectification of ancient evil, but it scarcely can be claimed that the Protestant churches have been important either in arousing public conscience to strike down the wrong or to support the decision once rendered.

To take an example from the economic sphere, the laws and

constitutional interpretations governing corporate law are similarly archaic and ill-fitted to maintain justice in industrial society. The corporation as a "legal person" has grown to national and international proportions, involving a vast body of extra-legal custom and practice utterly beyond the scope of local or state law and usually subject only to the spotty surveillance of national law and patriotic purpose. Whole sections of our economic life are a jungle, operating in the conditions of anarchy but slightly restrained by fortuitous expressions of an occasional public conscience.

In the midst of this scene of unplanned obsolescence the churches seldom serve as "the conscience of society." Rather, themselves committed to, and bound by, institutional patterns developed in a rural setting, they often find themselves suffering the indignity of painful and guilty irrelevance. In a society highly specialized and compartmentalized, the clergyman is almost the last generalist. In the seminary he is usually taught the importance of a neighborliness appropriate to a rural community where families have resided for generations, knowing their neighbors and their problems and concerns. He is usually taught that the church he is being trained to serve should be an integrative force and indeed the center of that community, and that he should be a leader in pulling the community together. He graduates to find himself in midstream in a highly mobile population, in which one out of four Americans has changed the state of his residence since World War II. Many, if not most, of his parishioners do not even know the names— let alone the problems and concerns—of those who live across the street or in the same apartment building. He finds that the Church is no longer the center of a community, that in fact the "community" as he understands it no longer exists—either as a geographical entity or as a focus of true interpersonal relations (*Gemeinschaft*).

If, on graduation, the seminarian is sent to a rural or village appointment, he finds himself on a crossroads leading to the nearest big city: his people commute long miles to work or to play, and like them he passes numbers of vacant store-fronts on his way to shop in the city. The county or consolidated school has removed even the education of the children from local influence. If he is appointed to the city, he finds a wasteland (or so it seems) from which the economic, social, and political leaders flee to the suburbs when working hours are over. If he follows them to the suburbs, as the churches have been doing for two generations, he finds himself the chaplain of their leisure-time activity. No wonder Protestant clergymen are breaking down!

In the city churches which survive by attracting people from many miles away in the suburbs, and in many churches which have followed the flight from the city to the suburbs, a type of social program has often been kept alive by rigidly maintaining old forms of words and acts. Consider the atavistic style of many laymen's organizations. How often does the men's society of the larger church consist of a club in which men who have moved to the city and made good strive to recover the emotional experience of the boyhood days down on the farm—by repeating the old phrases, singing the old songs, and calling by the first name others whose last names he has little interest in learning? And how often do laymen well-trained as doctors, lawyers, administrators, civil servants, salesmen, and so on, resist furiously any effort on the part of the clergy to carry them beyond the eighth-grade level of a sentimental, subjective, anti-intellectual, and essentially adolescent style of religion!

Those traditions which have a great heritage of sacramental life, such as those of the Episcopalians and the Lutherans, are in some respects less vulnerable than those of the Free Church tradition with their strong emphasis upon spontaneity and present consensus.[1] The disciplines of frequent communion and common prayer, set in the covenant which links together many generations of the faithful, are educative forces in themselves! Nevertheless, with the exception of significant experiments such as the Detroit Industrial Mission, East Harlem Protestant Parish and its affiliates in the central-city work, the churches are running away from the city—and the churches of rich liturgical tradition have shared in the rout. Yet, as John Osman has pointed out, "The logic of America is the city." [2] And to serve the Great City, American Protestantism needs a radically new vision of its mission and of the world it is called to serve.

## THE PRIMITIVIST MYTH

In a classical treatment of the problem, Truman B. Douglass has suggested that the "radical inability" of the churches "to penetrate the culture of modern cities" is due to

. . . an anti-urban bias which has become almost a point of dogma in American Protestantism. Many leading Protestants genuinely feel that a permanent and deadly hostility exists between urban man and those who are loyal to the Christian faith and ethic; that village ways of life are somehow more acceptable to God than city ways.[3]

Theologians who reject the romantic myth about rural life, a myth based on an attitude to technical advance which is called "primitivism," have endeavored to show that it is rooted in a misreading and mistranslation of biblical imperatives. The Bible does not compel us synthetically to reclaim the supposed virtues of rural and village life! It is my contention that the primitivist myth, so deeply engrained in American Protestantism, is the legitimate fruit of a studied misinterpretation of the course of religion in American history.

Deep in the mind-set of our churches is the memory of the "good old days" when America was a Christian (i.e., Protestant) nation.[4] For half of our history we did indeed have established churches in all the major colonies save one; and even Pennsylvania severely disadvantaged Jews, Unitarians, and Catholics. During this period the state churches of New England and the southern colonies were faithfully patterned after customs and legal arrangements peculiar to European Christendom. At the time of the Declaration of Independence, out of 3.6 million population only about twenty thousand were Roman Catholics and about six thousand were Jews; the rest were officially Protestant. In the period 1774-1833, with the breakup of compulsory affiliation, church membership fell to its true proportion—variously estimated between 5 per cent and 10 per cent of the people. Affiliation was higher in the North, lower in the South; in Georgia in 1798, out of a population of eighty thousand, less than five hundred were on any church rolls.

Confronted by this challenge, the American churchmen developed the institutions of mass evangelism which have shaped our religious life to the present day. In "the Great Century of Christian Missions," during which the Bible was translated and the gospel preached in more tongues by far than ever before, missions were nowhere more successful than in North America. Today, rightly conceived, the identity of the American churches is with the Younger Churches of the other great mission fields —in Africa, Asia, and the islands of the sea. Our whole style of life and work, from the camp meetings through radio and TV preaching, and including also our tradition of Christian social concern,[5] was created by mass evangelism. Today we stand at the high tide of the greatest mass accessions on a voluntary basis in two thousand years of church history, with 70 per cent of the population on the church rolls and 96 per cent of all Americans fourteen years of age and older claiming to be affiliated.

This is our true and glorious heritage. The very denominations which grew to great strength in America during this period—Baptists, Methodists, and Disciples/Christians—are characteristically revival churches. Yet, such is the persistence of attractive images, the same preachers who carried the Word to the masses helped to perpetuate the myth of a once-Christian America. Like Tacitus, who tried to shame his dissolute Roman contemporaries by portraying the Teutonic tribesmen as far more heroic and their women as far more beautiful and moral than they really were, the preachers tried to shame their contemporaries back into the churches by exaggerating the virtue of early Christian America and her sturdy yeomen. At its worst, Protestant primitivism has encouraged reactionary nativist crusades like the Know-Nothing Party—with the vicious anti-Catholicism, anti-Semitism, anti-intellectualism, anti-foreign sentiment which characterized it. A good deal of the resistance to equitable electoral reapportionment, incidentally, is justified in this way. At its best, the myth of a lost rural and Protestant Eden has rendered our churches impotent to meet the present given fact: the emergence of an industrialized and overwhelmingly urban America.

"*Religion today is challenged to create an urban civilization.*"[6] The great cities of the ancients centered in religious symbols. Medieval civilization found its highest moments in the life of urbane and humane man, with his cities built about cathedrals of worship and learning. What will our metropolitan areas be like if the great traditions of our society (*Gesellschaft*) —Catholic, Jewish, and Protestant—continue their present stampede from the ever enlarging wasteland of the Inner City? Do they not share the guilt for the wasteland?

## A NEW CONCEPT OF "COMMUNITY"

When the farm- or village-dweller migrates to the city he is initially overcome by the sense of isolation, of *anomie*. He misses the familiar ways of his former home, where neighborliness was a remembered—if not always practiced—virtue, and people were known and judged as persons. If he slips into the easy pattern of a highly mobile society[7] and accepts "quick-belongingness" as a substitute for realized interpersonal relations, he may never accept the city at all where he is condemned, as it were, to earn a living. His ruralist image of the city will condemn him to the very atomism and brokenness of relationships which he resents. If he participates in success, he will settle for a system of status based on symbols rather than on face-to-face encounter—house, car, job title, boat, etc.[8] If he participates in failure, he will show a low level of social and political concern, carry a negative image (hostility) toward the people living in proximity to him, be more prone to divorce, insanity, suicide, delinquency. In either case he will miss the most wonderful thing about the city: that it is a coagulating force for civilization, that its specialization presents a possibility of culture and liberty and fulfillment beyond the reach of less sophisticated and leisure-creating social organizations. More than that, he will live out his loneliness without ever seeing that the city in fact affords a richness of "community" quite beyond the capacity of more primitive social groupings.

The resident in the Great City is not, in fact, condemned to *anomie* unless he condemns himself by blindness or resentment. For the Great City is a complex network of many communities, not so much based on geographical propinquity as on vocational and professional identification. The city-dweller rarely knows, to be sure, the people who live on the same street or in the same apartment building. In the rural community, by contrast, everyone knows his neighbor's problems, concerns, economic status, personality potential—and, more than that, he knew his parents and grandparents and went to school and church with his uncles and his cousins and his aunts. The village, threatened in its time by the outside world, based its defense mechanisms on such knowledge; on the positive side, pulpit and voluntary civic groups stressed the virtues of the good neighbor—visiting the sick, aiding the needy, sponsoring the gifted child, caring for the orphan and indigent. In the specialized life of the city some of these activities are still the object of occasional campaigns—usually aimed at financial support for programs by trained personnel. Voluntary initiative by the untrained is not only rare; in some fields (e.g., care of orphans) it is illegal as well.

But communities are there, in great number, and within them the person of imagination and dedication can do great good. The communities of the Great City, which hold it together in a complex network of life relationships, are primarily vocational and professional. The bankers know each other, and so do the barbers. The taxi drivers know each other. The teachers know each other, and so do the preachers. And so it goes, with special magazines for dentists and others for lawyers. When a promising young sales manager is transferred from Memphis to the Chicago office, his friends will read about it in the trade journal and talk about it at lunch. He does not disappear from sight or from their awareness. The steelworker in Pittsburgh feels more identity with the steelworker in Gary and Montgomery than with those who live in the same section of his city. The doctor in Newark is certainly more closely tied to the doctors in San Francisco than to the public at large. Of course, there is the tendency for those who do a certain kind of work to seek out their peers in choosing a place of residence. But even here the controlling factor remains the new style of "community" identification: vocational and professional, and only secondarily geographical.

The importance of the new pattern of identification in the forming of attitudes, shaping of value judgments, inspiring of motivations, and defining the extent and limits of altruism has been documented in considerable detail by such pioneers of social psychology as Karl Mannheim[9] and Kurt Lewin.[10] For pointers on the importance of the new "we-groups" in industrial society, and new ways of communicating the gospel in the new setting, we may refer to the work of the Evangelical Academies and Lay Institutes. Dr. Eberhard Mueller, founder and leader of the adult education center at Bad Boll near Stuttgart, has discussed the issue in his writings.[11] And at Bad Boll, Kerk en Wereld near Utrecht, Loccum near Hannover, Tutzing near Munich, Boldern near Zurich, and several dozen other centers now scattered through central Europe and around the world, programs and specialized staffs have been developed to minister to the people in the new-style communities. At the First General Assembly of the World Council of Churches

(Amsterdam, 1948) and the Second Assembly (Evanston, 1954), the work of these centers of lay training was praised as pre-eminent in social evangelism and in recovering the ministry of the whole people of God.

Since the work of the local church, whether "parish" or "gathered community," is still conceived in geographical terms, the word applied to the new style of community has come to be "para-parish" (*Para-Gemeinde*). Here, parallel to the traditional local church and like it as a focus of Christian community, is a style of work of enormous importance to the civilizing of the Great City and its reintegration about religious symbols. To realize its potential, once we have abandoned the imagery of romantic ruralism and accepted the given factors of the place and time where we are called to work, requires a radical retooling of the concept of the general ministry, the program of theological education in our seminaries, and the staff arrangements in the representative ministry.

## THE GENERAL MINISTRY

A recent area survey showed many of the local churches with from 56 per cent to 66 per cent of the membership recent, and one-third to one-half of them coming from churches of other denominations in the process of moving place of residence. Two recent state surveys showed that two out of three who moved chose their new church home on other bases than confessional or liturgical loyalty. Their choices were functional: young couples would look for a lively Quest Club, parents of young children would search for a nearby church with a good Cradle Roll or begining Sunday School, older couples might look for an interesting preacher, etc. Quite evidently this free crossing of denominational lines has implications for inter-church relations which denominational leaders are seldom eager to consider. Quite evidently, too, high mobility is a denominational as well as a geographical factor. Most impor-tant of all, high mobility combined with the style of leadership developed during a century and a half of mass evangelism has tended to diminish the significance of the general ministry and to enhance the isolation of the stated clergy.

Yet there is a ministry which is shared by every Christian by virtue of the ordination of his baptism. The isolation of the clergy, combined with the virtual restriction of church pro-grams to matters of individual and familial piety, has removed whole areas of social existence from the claims of the Lordship of Jesus Christ. Properly conceived, there are no reservations apart from the "crown rights of the King." As the men of Barmen put it succinctly in their statement of Christian opposi-tion to totalitarian Nazism (May, 1934), "We repudiate the false teaching that there are areas of our life in which we belong not to Jesus Christ but another lord, areas in which we do not need justification and sanctification through him." [12]

The renewal of lay initiative, which we see in such mani-festations of the general ministry of Christians as the *Kirchen-tag* and the Evangelical Academies, rests above all on the recovery of the Reformation doctrine of the calling (*vocatio/ Beruf*). Rightly conceived, the Christian on the hospital staff, in the courts of law, on the assembly line, does not have a mere "job," a way of making a living: he has a calling. As Luther put it, in enunciating the famous principle of "the priesthood of all believers," "A cobbler, a smith, a peasant . . . all alike are consecrated priests and bishops, and every man in his office may be useful and beneficial to the rest . . . just as the members of the body serve one another." [13]

In an exciting new translation of Ephesians 4:11 we read: "And his gifts were that some should be apostles, some prophets, some evangelists, some pastors and teachers, *in order to* equip the saints for the work of ministry. . . ." The ministry of all the saints is the ministry which has been neglected. The general priesthood does not mean "every man his own priest"; it means that every believer shares in the ministry and the responsibility. The isolation of the clergy and the reduction of much of the membership to the status of roving spectators has brought our churches in many situations very close to the Catharist heresy, in which the movement was divided into two groups: a small class of the elite, the *perfecti*, who obeyed the gospel; and a large mass whose function it was to admire them for doing it, the *admirantes*.

The revival of the general ministry of the whole people of God, so much the center of theological discussion and writing today, requires that the new-style communities based on vocation or profession should be penetrated and influenced by the evangelical concern. This means that the local church program, which has succumbed so completely to the familial motif— what Peter L. Berger has called "the second childrens' crusade" —should think far beyond the Cradle Roll, Junior and Senior departments, Men's Class and Women's Society, Couples' Class and High School Fellowship, to embrace and redeem the new-style communities of our industrial society. If there is nothing else offered, some who move may seek out attractive programs of individual and familial religion; but the statistics show a much lower church affiliation among the mobile than among those who stay put.

There are today places and programs where the clergy are not isolated, where they are the chaplains to the Christian *Laos* in their ministry in the world. The Evangelical Academies represent the major breakthrough, and they carry on a constant series of lay training conferences of three types: (1) conferences in the discussion method, a previously neglected art in the European state-churches; (2) theme conferences, on such matters as the Church and European Co-operation, the Church and Racial Tensions, Christian Faith and East-West Tensions—the type of conference long familiar in the American churches; (3) conferences and seminars of persons in the same professional or vocational grouping—lawyers, schoolteachers, young farmers, policemen, army officers, miners, post office employees, automobile workers, personnel managers, etc. It is this third type of work which can teach us the most about meeting the challenge of the Great City and the new-style communities. Here participants are helped to see that Christianity is not a matter of creative use of leisure time, set in the Sunday morning context and church language, but supremely a matter of concrete decision and daily living on the job.

To give but one example of the type of conference, Tutzing near Munich has held over forty institutes for policemen. What is the vocation of a policeman? What does he owe his fellow citizens not in uniform? What do they owe him? (According to Christian teaching over centuries he is entitled to the prayers of the faithful to sustain him in the lawful exercise of his duties.) What is law? (The policeman is not "the law" but an agent of it, and this he must not forget.) What are the foundations of justice in the Old Testament? Why have the churches always stood against anarchy and the jungle? Twenty years ago Germany had one of the most vicious police forces in the world. Today West Germany has one of the best. Of considerable influence in this achievement, in the recovery of morale and discipline, have been the Christian adult education centers. What might be the effect of imaginative Christian initiative in various sections of the United States, dealing with the same vocation and its problems?

In America, several conferences along vocational lines have been held at Yokefellow Institute, Richmond, Indiana, and under the auspices of the Board of Social Missions of the United Lutheran Church and also the Board of Education of the Presbyterian Church in the U.S. One of the great potentials of this approach is in the campus ministry, where the frustration of a religion purely individual shows itself most plainly in the reduction of campus religious groups to small clubs at the margin of affairs. At one university, four years ago, the joint campus ministry resolved to meet the problem head-on by dividing the field in a kind of "comity agreement": one chaplain concentrated on work with the School of Medicine, another with the School of Nursing, another with the College of Business Administration. Regular programs were developed which enlisted the participation of faculty and alumni as well as students, and for the first time Christian concerns were integrated with the real educational process. Other examples might be given, from conferences at Kirkridge, at Five Oaks Christian Centre, at Laymen's International (Washington Cathedral), at Parishfield, and at other centers. The movement is spreading rapidly, and once the traditional parochial mold is broken a whole new dimension of the general ministry is opened up. "Jobs" become "vocations," and the new-style communities are brought under the shadow of the Cross.

### THEOLOGICAL EDUCATION

At the 1959 annual meeting of the directors of the European lay institutes, Dr. Eberhard Mueller read a paper in which he pointed out the importance of discussion (*Gespräch*) in the life of the Church. He said that although trained as a Lutheran theologian to stress the Word and the sacraments as the carriers of the Christian movement, he had come to the conclusion that a third mark of the Church must be added: Discussion. In the fullness of time we were at a moment of transition in Church history, with lay people no longer content to accept with docility and obedience the decisions and orders of a trained class of canon lawyers and theologians. To accept involvement and responsibility, the laity had to be involved in the process of making the decisions by which they were to be bound.

This does not imply any denigration of the importance of theology, Old and New Testament, or Church history in the curriculum of our seminaries. But it means that the young pastors must be trained to make theology come alive in the mind of the Church, to bring the Bible into the midst of the communities of faith, to interpret Church history as the life of the whole Christian people—and not just as dramatic events in the chronicles of great emperors, princes, and churchmen. It means that above all the clergy must be trained to function as the chaplains rather than the rulers of the faithful. Practically, they must know how to work with small, discussion-sized groups, and how to participate in a sensitive way in a decision-making situation. Much of the present isolation of the clergy is due to a style of seminary training which armed "pul-piteers," men skilled in proclamation to large groups, but all too frequently incapable of functioning in face-to-face, nonauthoritarian relationships.

## STAFF ARRANGEMENTS

On a district basis, and sometimes in the multiple ministry of larger churches, staff can be reassigned to deal with the "para-parishes." There are in the city today many large churches employing several clergymen and directors of Christian education; their work is traditionally divided along the lines of individual and familial needs. At least one large church (Highland Park Methodist Church, Dallas, Texas) has recently set aside one minister to work exclusively with the new-style communities. Retreats are being held with lawyers, doctors, insurance sales-men, real estate people, etc. A local church which has ninety doctors on its rolls has already a small *ecclesiola in ecclesia*. The only question is whether it will continue to address them and other laymen in the generality, or begin to lead a discussion involving concrete decisions by real people. At the present time it is plain enough that the communities which control the laymen's actions are unevangelized and largely unbaptized.

From the group-ministry projects which have developed in some rural areas and in several inner-city experiments, we can learn a style of staff work appropriate to smaller churches co-operating within a given area. In the evangelism of social struc-tures, one member of the clergy can represent the group min-istry as chaplain to the doctors, another to the lawyers, another to the schoolteachers, etc. The major vocational groups in-volved will depend upon the social texture of the area. The point to begin is with a vocational census within the large church or group of churches; the agreement as to responsibility then follows on the vocational concentrations and the particular interests and talents of individual clergy. Not only the representative ministry is involved, however, for it is precisely here that—with the growing volume of late deciders for the ministry and the larger number of early retired—men and women not ordained can begin to share in the specialized ministries of which the New Testament speaks.

The curse of the life of the clergy is to have to spend working hours on all kinds of things for which they were not trained. With the renewal of the general ministry through the recovery of the laymen's vocations, the representative ministry can again concentrate on those matters for which it was intended and is to be trained.

At this point begins the recovery of ministry and the religious redemption of the neglected Great City.

## ⤜ EPILOGUE

In contemporary theological discussion, much attention is given to such concepts as "the ministry of the laity," "the scattered Church," "the vocation of Christians in daily work," "the mission of the Church to the world." Such phrases point in two directions—inwardly, to the uneasiness within the Church about our future in a world of theological change; outwardly, to a recognition of the action of God within that change. If churchmen are to be relevantly concerned about their ministry, they must begin by discerning the actions of the Lord of history within the midst of life itself. A new age has come into being, one in which the potential of inflicting limitless suffering is as real to men as the promise of a new abundance. That God has placed such potential in human hands is either a divine caprice of unbelievable cruelty—or a mark of infinite love and trust. The vocation of Christians in our day, as in any other, is to discern the love and justice and judgment of God in the life of the world, and to witness to his power. Within the disciplined discovery of the action of God in the world of economic, social, and political life will emerge the patterns of church life appropriate to the new era.

# ➤ NOTES

KENNETH E. BOULDING          The Society of Abundance

1. Adam Smith, *The Wealth of Nations* (New York: E. P. Dutton, Everyman's Library), p. 10.


JOHN V. P. LASSOE, JR.          Man and Society
                                in the New Era

1. Gerald W. Johnson, *The Man Who Feels Left Behind* (New York: William Morrow and Co., 1961), p. 169.
2. William H. Whyte, Jr., "Urban Sprawl," *The Exploding Metropolis* (Garden City, N.Y.: Doubleday and Co., 1958), pp. 115 ff.
3. Scott Greer, *The Emerging City: Myth and Reality* (Glencoe, Ill.: The Free Press, 1962), pp. 166 ff.
4. C. Wright Mills, *The Power Elite* (New York: Oxford University Press, 1957), p. 306.
5. Erich Fromm, *The Art of Loving* (New York: Harper & Row, 1956), pp. 13 ff.
6. Peter Drucker, *Landmarks of Tomorrow* (New York: Harper & Row, 1957), p. 258.
7. William L. C. Wheaton, "The Two Cultures and the Urban Revolution," paper delivered at The National Conference on Urban Life, Washington, D.C., 1962.

8. Michael Harrington, *The Other America: Poverty in the United States* (New York: Macmillan Company, 1962), p. 2.

9. Conference on Economic Progress, *Poverty and Deprivation in the United States* (Washington, D.C.: CEP, 1962), pp. 67, 71.

10. Margaret Mead, "The Impact of Automation on Ethics and Culture," *The Impact of Automation,* proceedings of a Conference on Automation, 1957.

11. Fromm, *op. cit.,* pp. 14 ff.

ARTHUR E. WALMSLEY          The Mission of the Church
                           in the New Era

1. E. R. Wickham, "The Encounter of the Christian Faith and Modern Technological Society," *Ecumenical Review* (April, 1959), p. 265.

2. A. A. Berle, Jr., *Economic Power and the Free Society* (New York: The Fund for the Republic, 1957), p. 14.

3. "The Common Christian Responsibility Towards Areas of Rapid Social Change in Asia, Africa, and Latin America" (World Council of Churches, Dept. on Church and Society, 1956), p. 36.

4. "Dilemma and Opportunities: Christian Action in Rapid Social Change, Report of an International Ecumenical Study Conference" (World Council of Churches, Dept. on Church and Society, 1959), p. 45.

5. The public statements of Pope John XXIII, notably the encyclical *Pacem in Terris,* increasingly hold out the possibilities of a rapprochement between Roman Catholics and others in the area of collective action on social problems, and a move in the direction of accepting religious pluralism. *Pacem in Terris* declares: "The doctrinal principles outlined in this document . . . provide Catholics with a vast field in which they can meet and come to an understanding both with Christians separated from this Apostolic See, and also with human beings who are not enlightened by faith in Jesus Christ, but who are also endowed with the light of reason and with a natural and operative honesty . . . It can happen, then, that a drawing nearer together or a meeting for the attainment of some practical end, which was formerly deemed inopportune or unproductive, might now or in the future be considered

opportune and useful. But to decide whether this moment has arrived, and also to lay down the ways and degrees in which work in common might be possible for the achievement of economic, social, cultural and political ends which are honorable and useful: these are the problems which can only be solved with the virtue of prudence . . . Therefore, as far as Catholics are concerned, this decision rests primarily with those who live and work in the specific sectors of human society in which those problems arise, always, however, in accordance with the principles of the natural law, with the social doctrine of the church, and with the directives of ecclesiastical authority." In the new countries, at least, Rome is today prepared to discard the shopworn Christendom concept of Church and state.

6. Denis Munby, *The Idea of a Secular Society* (London: Oxford University Press, 1963), pp. 14-15, offers a definition of a secular society which fits the American situation today.

7. Romano Guardini, *Power and Responsibility* (1961), p. xiii.

8. In a keynote address delivered to the National Study Conference on the Church and Economic Life, Pittsburgh, Nov. 8, 1962.

9. William Temple, *What Christians Stand for in the Secular World* (London, SCM, 1944), p. 14.

10. Part II of this book examines two threats to the new society. Chapter 5 considers the failure of the West to solve the problem of distribution of wealth in a world rising to shake off its poverty. Chapter 6 deals with the arms race, the most striking example of our dehumanization and the costliest economic incentive in human history.

11. Klaus von Bismarck, E. V. Mathew, and Mollie Batten, "The Laity: The Church in the World," printed in the *Ecumenical Review* (January, 1962), p. 205.

12. Part III of this book considers three crucial questions confronting the Church in the abundant society. Chapter 7 concerns the theological revolution which must take place with respect to our understanding of human worth and accomplishment as society moves from an economy of production to one of consumption. Chapter 8 discusses the problem which the institutional Church faces as the state increasingly assumes responsibility for the ministry to human needs. Chapter 9 considers the shape which the formal ministry and corporate life of the Church must assume to minister to men in the new society.

## CAMERON P. HALL          Leisure in the New Era

1. Sebastian de Grazia, *Of Time, Work and Leisure* (New York: The Twentieth Century Fund, 1962.

2. Walter Buckingham, *Automation: Its Impact on Business and People* (New York: Harper & Row, 1961), p. 175.

3. Statement by the AFL-CIO Executive Council, August 14, 1962.

4. *Fortune,* June, 1959.

5. Alan Richardson, *The Biblical Doctrine of Work* (London: Student Christian Movement Press, 1952), p. 53. It will be apparent how much in accord was the Puritan view of work and leisure with that in the Bible.

## ROSS M. ROBERTSON          Stewardship: Private and Public

1. For example, most Protestant churches count as members only those who have attained full membership, 90 to 95 per cent of their reported members being thirteen years of age and over. On the other hand, Roman Catholics count all baptized persons as members, and more than one-fifth of their membership consists of children less than thirteen.

2. C. Luther Fry, *Recent Social Trends in the United States,* II (New York: The McGraw-Hill Book Co., 1933), 1020. Readers wishing to examine methods and data should consult U.S. Bureau of the Census, *Census of Religious Bodies,* 1929, I, "Summary and Detailed Tables," 16.

3. *Giving USA 1962* (New York: American Association of Fund-Raising Counsel, Inc., 1962), p. 28.

4. Alfred de Grazia and Ted Gurr, *American Welfare* (New York: New York University Press, 1961, p. 100.

5. For slightly different interpretations of these figures see Fry, *op. cit.,* pp. 1028-1030, and H. Paul Douglass and Edmund de S. Brunner, *The Protestant Church as a Social Institution* (New York: Harper & Row, 1935), pp. 206-208. The reader will note that *expenditures* rather than *receipts* are taken as synonymous with *giving,* largely for the reason that expenditure data are easier to come by. It should be remembered that expenditures include substantial amounts of "deficit" financing of plant and equipment purchases.

6. See de Grazia and Gurr, *op. cit.*, pp. 100-101, and *Giving USA 1962*, p. 28.

7. Summaries of these programs may be found in de Grazia and Gurr, *op. cit.*, pp. 101-136, and in *Social Work Year Book 1960*, edited by Russell H. Kurtz (New York: National Association of Social Workers, 1960), pp. 136-141, 338-343, 441-450.

8. *Social Work Year Book 1960*, p. 442.

9. It is almost impossible to estimate closely the charitable contributions of religious organizations before 1910. In a recently published work, historian Robert H. Bremner sketches the history of philanthropy in the United States and scarcely mentions churches. See his *American Philanthropy* (Chicago: The University of Chicago Press, 1960). For an impressionistic and descriptive treatment, but one yielding little in the way of quantitative information, see also Frank Dekker Watson, *The Charity Organization Movement in the United States* (New York: Macmillan Company, 1922).

10. These data are taken from series H 1-29, Social Welfare Expenditures Under Civilian Public Programs: 1890-1956, in U.S. Bureau of the Census, *Historical Statistics of the United States*, p. 193. For the sources of the early estimates see p. 189.

11. A definition of welfare programs that includes education may seem too broad for analytical purposes, but the use of this concept is dictated by the need for a generally accepted time series.

12. John Kenneth Galbraith's best seller, *The Affluent Society* (Boston: Houghton, Mifflin Co., 1958), gave general credence to the view that only "pockets" of poverty persist in the United States. For a typical parroting of this nonsense, see Albert Terrell Rasmussen's "Stewardship in an Economy of Abundance," *Stewardship in Contemporary Theology* (New York: Association Press, 1960), pp. 228-252.

## FRANKLIN H. LITTELL    The Recovery of Ministry

1. See the significant discussion of "parish" and "gathered community," as they relate to the failure of Protestantism in the city, by Howard C. Hageman, "The Theology of the Urban Church," reprinted in Robert Lee, ed., *Cities and Churches: Readings on the Urban Church* (Philadelphia: Westminster Press, 1962), pp. 331-48.

2. John Osman, "A City Is a Civilization," reprinted in Robert Lee, ed., *op. cit.*, p. 75.

3. Truman B. Douglass, "The Job the Protestants Shirk," reprinted in Robert Lee, ed., *op. cit.*, p. 88; see also the essay by Peter L. Berger in the same volume, pp. 66-71: "Community in Modern Urban Society."

4. A summary of the argument presented in Franklin H. Littell, Anchor Book, *From State to Pluralism* (New York: Doubleday & Co., 1962).

5. See the significant study by Timothy L. Smith, *Revivalism and Social Reform* (Nashville: Abingdon Press, 1957).

6. John Osman, *loc. cit.*

7. Paul S. Minear, ed., *The Nature of the Unity We Seek* (St. Louis: Bethany Press, 1958), Sec. 9, "The Mobility of the Population," and Appendix I, "The Impact of Mobility as It Affects the Work of the Churches in the USA," pp. 246-54, 275-88.

8. See Vance Packard, *The Status Seekers* (New York: Pocket Books, 1961), Chaps. 8 and 17.

9. See especially *Ideology and Utopia* (New York: Harcourt, Brace & Co., 1952); also *Man and Society in an Age of Reconstruction* (New York: Harcourt, Brace & Co., 1951).

10. Kurt Lewin, *Resolving Social Conflicts: Selected Papers on Group Dynamics* (New York: Harper & Row, 1948).

11. Eberhard Mueller, *Die Welt ist anders geworden* (Hamburg: Furche-Verlag, 1953); see also my *The German Phoenix* (New York: Doubleday & Co., 1960), Chap. V.

12. *The German Phoenix*, p. 186.

13. Note the argument in the "Letter to the Christian Nobility of the German Nation," *Three Treatises* (Philadelphia: Muhlenberg Press, 1943).